Letts
Study Aids

J   Eyre

arlotte Brontë

Guide written and developed by
John Mahoney and Stewart Martin

Charles Letts & Co Ltd
London, Edinburgh & New York

First published 1987
by Charles Letts & Co Ltd
Diary House, Borough Road, London SE1 1DW
Reprinted 1988

Illustration: Peter McClure

Stewart Martin is an Honours graduate of Lancaster University, where he read English
and Sociology. He has worked both in the UK and abroad as a writer, a teacher, and an
educational consultant. He is married with three children, and is currently deputy
headmaster at Ossett School in West Yorkshire.

John Mahoney has taught English for twenty years. He has been head of English
department in three schools and has wide experience of preparing students at all levels
for most examination boards. He has worked both in the UK and North America
producing educational books and computer software on English language and literature.
He is married with three children and lives in Worcestershire.

British Library Cataloguing in Publication Data
Mahoney, John
Jane Eyre: Charlotte Brontë: guide.
(Guides to literature)
1. Brontë, Charlotte. Jane Eyre
I. Title   II. Martin, Stewart
III. Brontë, Charlotte. Jane Eyre   IV. Series
823'.8   PR4167.J5

ISBN 0 85097 774 6

Printed and bound in Great Britain by
Charles Letts (Scotland) Ltd

Contents

To the student

This study companion to your English literature text acts as a guide to the novel or play being studied. It suggests ways in which you can explore content and context, and focuses your attention on those matters which will lead to an understanding, appreciative and sensitive response to the work of literature being studied.

Whilst covering all those aspects dealt with in the traditional-style study aid, more importantly, it is a flexible companion to study, enabling you to organize the patterns of study and priorities which reflect your particular needs at any given moment.

Whilst in many places descriptive, it is never prescriptive, always encouraging a sensitive personal response to a work of literature, rather than the shallow repetition of others' opinions. Such objectives have always been those of the good teacher, and have always assisted the student to gain high grades in 16+ examinations in English literature. These same factors are also relevant to students who are doing coursework in English literature for the purposes of continual assessment.

The major part of this guide is the 'Commentary' where you will find a detailed commentary and analysis of all the important things you should know and study for your examination. There is also a section giving practical help on how to study a set text, write the type of essay that will gain high marks, prepare coursework and a guide to sitting examinations.

Used sensibly, this guide will be invaluable in your studies and help ensure your success in the course.

Charlotte Brontë

Charlotte Brontë was born in 1816, the third of six children. When she was four years old her father became parson of Haworth and the family moved to this village which is near Keighley in Yorkshire. The countryside around Haworth is bleak moorland and the climate is harsh. The toll it took on the Brontë family was enormous. Charlotte outlived all her sisters and her brother, although she herself died before the age of forty.

Charlotte's mother died in 1821 and the children were brought up by their father and an aunt who had come up from Cornwall to look after them. At the age of seven Charlotte followed her elder sisters, Maria and Elizabeth, to Cowan Bridge School. Here the girls were to receive a 'plain and useful' education but, partly as a result of damp conditions and poor food, Maria and Elizabeth became ill and were sent home, where they died of tuberculosis. Charlotte and Emily, who were by now also at the school, left and returned to Haworth.

For the next five years the four remaining children were educated at home by their father. They led a richly imaginative life, inventing their own secret world and writing miniature books about make-believe places called *Gondal* and *Angria*.

When she was fifteen, Charlotte was sent away to Roe Head School where she stayed for eighteen months. She returned home to teach her younger sisters, Emily and Anne, and then in 1835 she went back to Roe Head as a teacher. Emily and Anne attended the school as pupils. Their father's intention was that they should become governesses, the only respectable occupation open to genteel but poor young ladies. After three years Charlotte left the school to take up various posts as a governess but she was never happy. The sisters planned to open a school of their own and towards this end Charlotte and Emily went to Brussels to improve their French. Charlotte remained there, at the Pensionnat Héger, for two years.

In 1844 Charlotte went back to Haworth and the girls were ready to open their school. However their brother, Branwell, brought disgrace to the family with his drinking and drug-taking so the girls were forced to give up their plans. Instead they decided to try to get some of their poems published. Under the pseudonyms of Currer, Ellis and Acton Bell a volume of poetry was published. Although it met with no great success they continued to write, this time concentrating on novels. In 1846 Emily submitted *Wuthering Heights*, Anne *Agnes Grey* and Charlotte *The Professor* to publishers. The first two were accepted for publication but Charlotte's work was rejected. Asked to send in something else, Charlotte began writing *Jane Eyre*, which she rapidly finished. Accepted and published in October 1847 under the pseudonym Currer Bell, it was very well received. In order to allay the suspicion that all three works were written by the same author the Brontë sisters revealed their identities.

The happiness of their success was short-lived for in the following year great tragedy struck the family. Branwell died in October, followed by his sister Emily in December. Anne, too, became ill and, despite sea visits to improve her health, she died in Scarborough in the following May. Notwithstanding her grief Charlotte returned to writing and completed her third novel, *Shirley*.

Her position in literary circles was by now established and during the next five years she made frequent journeys to London and made the acquaintance of such literary figures as Thackeray, Matthew Arnold, and Harriet Martineau, as well as Mrs Gaskell, who later wrote her biography. During this time she wrote *Villette* which drew particularly on her experiences in Belgium.

Although she enjoyed her visits to London she had no desire to settle there. She still lived in Haworth with her elderly father. In 1854 at the age of thirty-eight she married the Reverend Arthur Bell Nicholls, who had previously been her father's curate. (She had previously turned down proposals of marriage from Henry Nussey in March 1839, and from Mr Bryce in July of the same year.) The marriage lasted less than a year as Charlotte Brontë died of tuberculosis in March 1855.

Jane Eyre is Charlotte Brontë's most famous novel, and was based on her own experiences of life. That is not to say it was autobiographical, but that she wrote about things she knew well. Cowan Bridge School was no doubt the inspiration for Lowood School, and it is said that Helen Burns was based on her sister Maria. Her distaste for teaching shows through in the novel, as does her strong belief in the independence of women. But to say that the book is concerned only with these things is to ignore the great imaginative powers that have created a strong, well-written, closely detailed narrative with diverse, well-drawn characters, the most interesting of all, of course, being Jane Eyre herself.

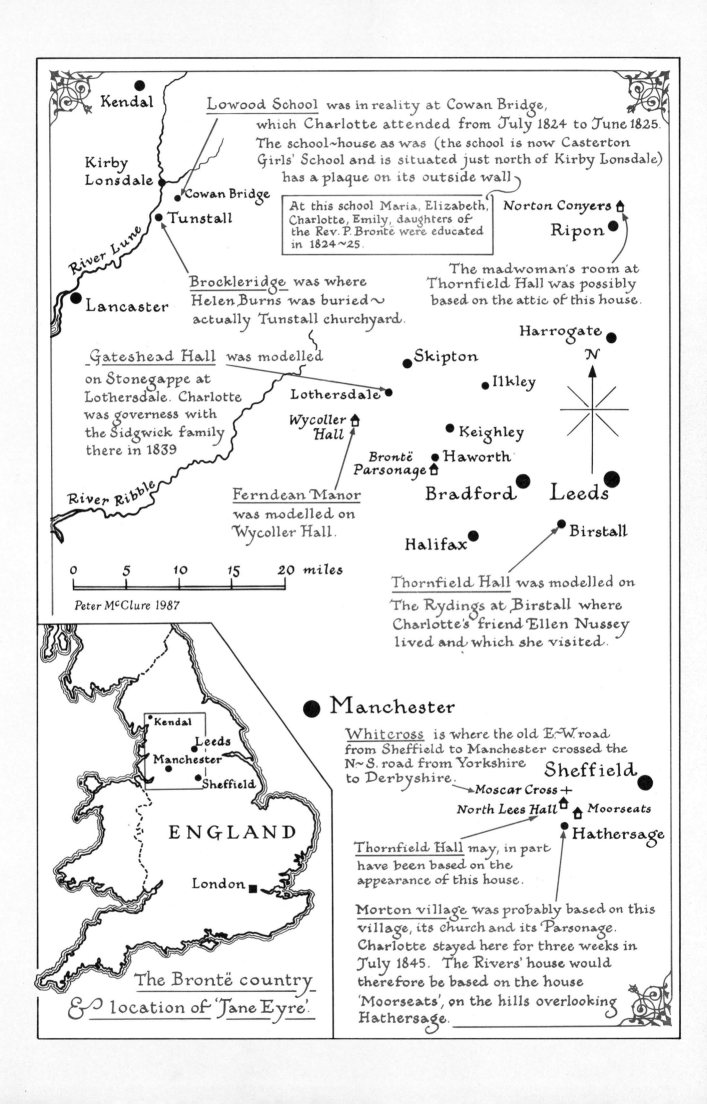

Kendal

Kirby Lonsdale

Cowan Bridge

Tunstall

River Lune

Lancaster

Lowood School was in reality at Cowan Bridge, which Charlotte attended from July 1824 to June 1825. The school~house as was (the school is now Casterton Girls' School and is situated just north of Kirby Lonsdale) has a plaque on its outside wall

At this school Maria, Elizabeth, Charlotte, Emily, daughters of the Rev. P. Brontë were educated in 1824~25.

Norton Conyers

Ripon

The madwoman's room at Thornfield Hall was possibly based on the attic of this house.

Brockleridge was where Helen Burns was buried ~ actually Tunstall churchyard.

Gateshead Hall was modelled on Stonegappe at Lothersdale. Charlotte was governess with the Sidgwick family there in 1839

River Ribble

Harrogate

N

Skipton

Ilkley

Lothersdale

Wycoller Hall

Keighley

Brontë Parsonage

Haworth

Ferndean Manor was modelled on Wycoller Hall.

Bradford

Leeds

Halifax

Birstall

Thornfield Hall was modelled on The Rydings at Birstall where Charlotte's friend Ellen Nussey lived and which she visited.

0   5   10   15   20 miles

Peter McClure 1987

Kendal

Leeds

Manchester

Sheffield

ENGLAND

London

The Brontë country & location of 'Jane Eyre'.

Manchester

Whitcross is where the old E~W road from Sheffield to Manchester crossed the N~S. road from Yorkshire to Derbyshire.

Sheffield

Moscar Cross +

North Lees Hall

Moorseats

Hathersage

Thornfield Hall may, in part, have been based on the appearance of this house.

Morton village was probably based on this village, its church and its Parsonage. Charlotte stayed here for three weeks in July 1845. The Rivers' house would therefore be based on the house 'Moorseats', on the hills overlooking Hathersage.

Understanding Jane Eyre
An exploration of the major topics and themes in the novel

Summaries of themes

Aspects of style

Charlotte Brontë adopted the narrator technique of relating the story. This is both an effective way of engaging the reader's sympathy and attention, because we all love to be told stories, and it is also a method of writing which allows the author to use irony as a way of satirizing certain characters. This is done by describing characters from the personalized viewpoint of the heroine or hero in the story. The narrator technique also allows Charlotte Brontë to create mystery and hold the reader's interest by the use of suspense, usually via questions and conjecture on the part of the narrator.

Jane Eyre is a novel which has a stong Gothic flavour to it – the term refers to the 19th-century taste for blood-curdling, gruesome description, with special emphasis on strange wild creatures and vampires. Mary Shelley's *Frankenstein* is a good example of this kind of story. Such details as exist in *Jane Eyre* are included under this heading. There are other references in the novel which have a distinct 19th-century flavour to them and these have been pointed out at the appropriate places in the commentary. Rochester, for example, mentions phrenology, which was a popular science in Brontë's day, when it was thought by many that the study of the physical construction of the skull could reveal a person's character.

Throughout *Jane Eyre* a thoughtful reader will discover many subtle parallels and echoes, from telling touches like the author's use of the image of the tree as a symbol of life, to the name given to Rochester's dog who in many ways is indeed the 'pilot' who brings the hero and heroine together, through to larger structural devices. These devices are, like the imagery, often used in both a figurative and a dramatic way. Notice for example how the idea of a mirror recurs in the book. It is a symbol of the contrast between appearance and reality. The mirror image is not used to suggest an accurate representation of something. It is not that a mirror always grossly distorts whatever is seen in it – a mirror's reflections are more curious than that. Things seen in ordinary mirrors are subtly reversed. Brontë's use of the idea is to suggest the reflection (contrast) between characters, for we can see in St John a kind of mirror image of Mr Rochester; Blanche Ingram as a reflection of Jane and Mr Brocklehurst as an echo of Miss Temple. Notice also how Brontë uses images connected with light and dark to symbolize goodness and despair.

Charlotte Brontë deals with religious and social hypocrisy, the former personified by Mr Brocklehurst, the latter by Miss Ingram. As with many of the other themes and images in the novel, hypocrisy is highlighted by contrast, in the first place through the character of Miss Temple and in the second place throught the character of Jane.

Imagination is seen as a means of escape from stressful reality, in that it offers consolation and shelter from a hostile world. A good example of this appears in the way Brontë uses art. The function of art in the book is actually twofold; firstly as an outlet for the imagination, and secondly as a means of observing and describing in minute detail the physical qualities of the characters.

The role of education is fundamental to the development of the plot. Three different aspects are used and described – Lowood School, a charity boarding school for ladies; Adèle's education by a governess; and a small village elementary school. Each of the episodes dealing with these places is used by Brontë both to develop the plot and to reveal something about the characters involved. Brontë also uses the various facets of schooling to progress Jane's own education and to reveal, and thereby comment upon, something of the social attitudes of the day.

Appearances

The theme of appearances explores the difference between what seems to be the case and the reality. For example, it includes such things as the role that dress plays in establishing one person's image of another and also the significance of beauty as a social asset.

Bird

The image and attributes of birds is something which is frequently (but carefully) used by Brontë. It is used to describe both Jane and Mr Rochester. All the attributes of a bird are called upon at various times – its song, its size and its ability to fly.

Books

Throughout the novel the image of a book is used as a symbol of inspiration and comfort. It is also used to emphasize the contrast between Jane and Helen.

Class

This story is set against the class background of the 19th century, and certain aspects of this are pointedly used in the story – particularly in regard to attitudes towards the poor relation, education and marriage. As with different characters' attitudes towards money however, these things serve only as a backdrop for the main questions of the book.

Dreams

Dreams play an important role in the structure of the book because of their timing in the action of the story. Their interpretation adds to the feeling of suspense because they suggest the possible nature of future events; this is also related to the way the narrator technique is used (see 'Aspects of style', on page 9).

Environment

Often in the book there is a vital link between the mood of a character and that of a scene or the surroundings. This feature of the writing encompasses the weather, seasons and countryside. The atmosphere of each episode and our insight into each character is enhanced by reference to the outside world. This device was common in much of Gothic and Romantic literature, including poetry. The technical expression to describe this way of writing is to say that the author has made use of the 'pathetic fallacy'.

The term 'pathetic fallacy' was invented by the great 19th-century writer John Ruskin, who used it when objecting to the way in which some poets insisted on writing about inanimate objects or natural occurrences as though they had human feelings or could perform human actions. For example in *Jane Eyre* we can see how Brontë has used descriptions of the wind not only to suggest wild surroundings or tempests in nature, but also as an image of mental agitation in some of the characters. It is as though the world of nature had 'moods' like a real person and, further, that these moods tended to be roused as an echo of those of the actual people present. Water, for example, is used in *Jane Eyre* not only as a natural feature of landscape or weather, but also as a symbol of overwhelming emotion in characters. When writers use the 'pathetic fallacy' they are using a particular form of personification. Ruskin used the word 'pathetic' because the technique relies on the reader being aware of the presence of pathos – that is a feeling of sympathy or pity (pathos comes from the Greek word for 'suffering') – and the word 'fallacy' indicates that the suggested connection is essentially fallacious, or false.

Fire

Fire performs a dual symbolism in *Jane Eyre*. At times fire symbolizes comfort and well-being, whilst at other times it symbolizes passion. (See also 'Environment', above.)

Food

Food is often mentioned in close conjunction with 'Fire' (see page 10) to suggest or symbolize the presence of physical or emotional comfort. The mention of fire is also used carefully by Brontë as a contrast to other themes or images which have opposite emotional connotations – like the similes connected with stone for instance. A good example of this last device appears near the end of the commentary in connection with the emotional state and character of St John Rivers.

Independence

The importance of independence is one of the main themes of the book. It is concerned with exploring the need for people to be faithful to their characters or natures and to have the freedom to develop their faculties as they see fit. It is a matter of personal integrity. The conflicts this can cause are fully explored, such as the battles with family, with authority, with religion and with social custom.

Linked with the theme of independence there is a strong plea for what today we might classify as one aspect of human rights – in *Jane Eyre* the particular plea for equality relates to the situation of women. The emphasis is not so much on the need for equality of social opportunity, although there is regret expressed at the poverty of choice available to women, but for equality in personal relationships. Through the developing relationship between Jane and Mr Rochester we see that love and mutual respect, support and understanding, are possible in female-male relationships without the need for either partner to be dominant or subservient.

The themes of independence, equality and nature are dominant throughout the Gateshead and Lowood episodes of the book, where they are explored through an examination of the injustices which take place. A contrast is drawn between Jane's and Helen's attitudes to injustice, which illuminates both their characters. In a similar way, but much later on in the book, references to slavery occur when the themes of rebellion and independence are apparent, and the role of injustice is to emphasize and illustrate these larger themes – a good example is the relationship between Jane and St John Rivers. However, the theme rises in both of Jane's close relationships with men – for instance, look at how the wedding veil acts as both a dramatic device in the story and as a symbol of control in the relationship between Jane and Mr Rochester. The image of the mad Bertha Rochester tearing up the veil in Jane's bedchamber is therefore both powerful and complex.

Money features in *Jane Eyre* as a part of the theme of independence but its role in Jane's life is not exaggerated, nor is its worth regarded as very great. It is not, for example, as important as Jane's constant rebellion. Its role is to serve as background to the main concerns of the book and also to the struggles that arise as both Jane and other characters try to free themselves from the restraints of their natures.

Isolation

The theme of isolation is linked throughout the book with a character, usually Jane, being in the state of being unloved. On the occasions that Jane feels most lonely she is without friends.

Love

One of the major themes of the novel is the desire to love and be loved. The term extends further than romantic love to cover friendship, respect and affection. It is one of the driving forces in the life of the main character and is contrasted to many other kinds of love – love of social position, love of money, love of God, and so on.

Nature

One of the dominant themes of the book is the debate between Nature and Principle. The argument is about how far people should behave according to their natural inclinations and how far they should allow learnt principles to control them. This theme is explored in various contexts from Lowood, where it is personified in the contrasting characters of Jane and Helen, through to Thornfield, where Jane opts for principle over nature, to Moor House, where the debate is at its most explicit. Jane finally resolves the dilemma for herself. As part of the wider theme of nature the contrast in attitudes to death is shown in the characters of Helen and Jane. Notice that the idea of death as entry to another, better world does not go unchallenged.

Passion

Passion is the word used here to describe the strength of feeling between Jane and Mr Rochester. The struggle between passion and control dominates the middle section of the book. Although linked to the theme of nature it relates particularly to Jane, whose need for emotional control is due to social rather than religious pressures.

Stone

Images and references to various types and uses of stone are common, including 'marble' and 'pillar' and other architectural terms. The references to stone are usually used to denote lack of feeling.

Supernatural

The supernatural aspects of *Jane Eyre* are linked to other, more general, aspects of style (see above). The supernatural elements in the novel describe the 'other worldly' sides of characters and events. This theme is most apparent in the relationship between Jane and Mr Rochester where it emphasizes the spiritual nature of their love and adds a touch of mystery to Mr Rochester's character. It is not used in any directly religious sense.

Finding your way around the commentary

Each page of the commentary gives the following information:

1 A quotation from the start of each paragraph on which a comment is made, or act/scene or line numbers plus a quotation, so that you can easily locate the right place in your text.

2 A series of comments, explaining, interpreting, and drawing your attention to important incidents, characters and aspects of the text.

3 For each comment, headings to indicate the important characters, themes, and ideas dealt with in the comment.

4 For each heading, a note of the comment numbers in this guide where the previous or next comment dealing with that heading occurred.

Thus you can use this commentary section in a number of ways.

1 Turn to that part of the commentary dealing with the chapter/act you are perhaps revising for a class discussion or essay. Read through the comments in sequence, referring all the time to the text, which you should have open before you. The comments will direct your attention to all the important things of which you should take note.

2 Take a single character or topic from the list on page 14. Note the comment number next to it. Turn to that comment in this guide, where you will find the first of a number of comments on your chosen topic. Study it, and the appropriate part of your text to which it will direct you. Note the comment number in this guide where the next comment for your topic occurs and turn to it when you are ready. Thus, you can follow one topic right through your text. If you have an essay to write on a particular character or theme just follow the path through this guide and you will soon find everything you need to know!

3 A number of relevant relationships between characters and topics are listed on page 15. To follow these relationships throughout your text, turn to the comment indicated. As the previous and next comment are printed at the side of each page in the commentary, it is a simple matter to flick through the pages to find the previous or next occurrence of the relationship in which you are interested.

For example, you want to examine in depth the theme of class in the novel. Turning to the single topic list, you will find that this theme first occurs in comment 10. On turning to comment 10 you will discover a zero (0) in the place of the previous reference (because this is the first time that it has occurred) and the number 23 for the next reference. You now turn to comment 23 and find that the previous comment number is 10 (from where you have just been looking) and that the next reference is to comment 25, and so on throughout the text.

You also wish to trace the relationship between Rochester and independence throughout the novel. From the relationships list, you are directed to comment 102. This is the first time that both Rochester and independence are discussed together and you will find that the next time that this happens occurs in comment 103 (the 'next' reference for both Rochester and independence). On to comment 103, where you are directed to comment 104, and you will now discover that two different comment numbers are given for the subject under examination – numbers 105 and 145. This is because each character and theme are traced separately as well as together and you will have to continue tracing them separately until you finally come to comment 145 – the next occasion on which both Rochester and independence are discussed.

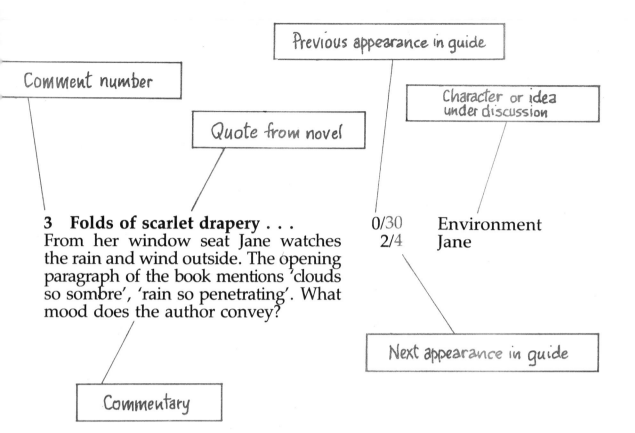

Comment number

Previous appearance in guide

Quote from novel

Character or idea under discussion

3   Folds of scarlet drapery . . .
From her window seat Jane watches the rain and wind outside. The opening paragraph of the book mentions 'clouds so sombre', 'rain so penetrating'. What mood does the author convey?

0/30   Environment
2/4   Jane

Next appearance in guide

Commentary

Single topics:

	Comment no:		Comment no:
Aspects of style	14	Adèle Varens	80
Appearances	1	Bertha Rochester	238
Bird	110	Bessie Leavens	5
Books	4	Blanche Ingram	6
Class	10	Diana and Mary	
Dreams	4	Rivers	259
Environment	3	Eliza Reed	29
Fire	13	Georgiana Reed	167
Food	38	Grace Poole	79
Independence	8	Helen Burns	40
Isolation	2	Jane Eyre	1
Love	16	John Reed	6
Nature	15	Miss Temple	6
Passion	81	Mr Brocklehurst	31
Stone	31	Mr Mason	141
Supernatural	14	Mr Rochester	76
		Mrs Fairfax	72
		Mrs Reed	2
		St John Rivers	264

Just as in many other works of fiction, several of the characters and themes in *Jane Eyre* are closely bound up with one another. There is considerable 'overlap' as far as relationships are concerned and you should not assume that because a particular relationship is not listed below it is not present in the novel, or is not important. This list of relationships is not exhaustive, nor is it meant to be. In the final analysis it is the understanding and interpretation which *you* draw from your reading which is most important. This list simply provides a useful jumping-off point for your own ideas.

Relationships:

			Comment no:
Helen Burns	and	Love	54
	and	Nature	44
	and	Jane Eyre	40
Jane Eyre	and	Appearances	1
	and	Bird	110
	and	Books	4
	and	Class	10
	and	Dreams	4
	and	Environment	3
	and	Fire	13
	and	Independence	8
	and	Isolation	2
	and	Love	16
	and	Nature	15
	and	Passion	81
	and	Supernatural	17
	and	John Reed	7
	and	Mr Rochester	87
	and	Mrs Reed	2
	and	St John Rivers	269
Mr Rochester	and	Appearances	99
	and	Environment	140
	and	Independence	102
	and	Love	88
	and	Nature	107
	and	Supernatural	94
	and	St John Rivers	330
St John Rivers	and	Nature	272
	and	Stone	273
Aspects of style	and	Appearances	33
	and	Dreams	97
Appearances	and	Love	16
Nature	and	Independence	15
	and	Love	45

Analysis chart

Important events

		1	2	3	4	5	6	7	8	9	10	11	12	13	14	15	16	17	18	19
	Event	Jane is living at Gateshead with her aunt	Jane is put into the red-room as a punishment	Mr Lloyd suggests sending Jane away to school	Mr Brocklehurst interviews Jane	Jane arrives at Lowood. She meets Miss Temple and Helen	Helen Burns and Jane become close friends	Mr Brocklehurst visits Lowood and humiliates Jane	Jane comes to prefer Lowood to Gateshead	The typhus epidemic – Helen dies	Miss Temple leaves Lowood. Jane leaves after meeting Bessie	Jane arrives at Thornfield and meets Adèle	Mr Rochester and Jane meet	Mr Rochester and Jane discuss her pictures	Mr Rochester's conversation confuses Jane	Rochester's bed is set on fire	Jane learns about Blanche Ingram	The houseparty arrives	Mr Mason arrives. The 'gypsy' tells the ladies' fortunes	Jane meets the 'gypsy' and discovers the truth
Chapter		1	2	3	4	5	6	7	8	9	10	11	12	13	14	15	16	17	18	19
Places	Gateshead	●	●	●	●	●														
	Lowood School					●	●	●	●	●	●									
	Thornfield Hall											●	●	●	●	●	●	●	●	●
	Moor House																			
	The School																			
	Ferndean																			
Themes	Aspects of style		●	●	●	●		●	●		●		●	●	●	●	●	●	●	●
	Appearances	●	●	●	●							●	●		●	●	●	●	●	
	Bird														●					
	Books	●		●		●													●	
	Class		●	●	●			●											●	
	Dreams	●	●						●				●	●		●				
	Environment	●			●	●	●			●		●				●			●	
	Fire		●		●		●		●			●	●			●				
	Food						●												●	
	Independence	●	●							●	●	●			●					●
	Isolation	●		●	●		●					●								
	Love		●		●		●		●	●			●		●	●		●	●	●
	Nature		●		●		●	●	●	●					●	●		●		●
	Passion												●			●				
	Stone				●															
	Supernatural		●									●	●	●		●				
Characters	Adèle Varens												●			●		●		
	Bertha Rochester																			
	Bessie Leavens	●	●	●	●															
	Blanche Ingram	●																	●	●
	Diana/Mary Rivers																			
	Eliza Reed				●															
	Georgiana Reed																			
	Grace Poole												●	●				●	●	
	Helen Burns						●	●	●	●	●									
	Jane	●	●	●	●	●	●	●	●	●	●	●	●	●	●	●	●	●	●	●
	John Reed	●																		
	Miss Temple	●				●		●	●		●									
	Mr Brocklehurst				●				●	●	●									
	Mr Mason																		●	
	Mr Rochester											●	●	●	●	●		●	●	●
	Mrs Fairfax											●								
	Mrs Reed	●	●		●															
	St John Rivers																			
Page in commentary on which chapter first appears		19	20	21	22	23	24	25	26	27	28	28	29	31	32	33	35	35	37	38

Important events

Chapter	Event
20	Mason is wounded and leaves Thornfield in secret
21	Jane is summoned to Gateshead – her aunt dies
22	Jane and Rochester meet again when she returns to Thornfield
23	Rochester confesses his feelings for Jane. The chestnut tree is split by lightning
24	Jane keeps Rochester at arm's length!
25	Jane sees the tree. She tells Rochester of her dreams
26	The marriage service is interrupted. Jane meets Bertha Rochester
27	Jane leaves Thornfield in secret
28	The Rivers family take pity on Jane and take her in
29	St John interviews Jane
30	St John asks Jane to become village schoolmistress. The Rivers' uncle dies
31	Miss Oliver and St John meet and Jane learns about his mission
32	Jane discusses with St John his feelings for Miss Oliver
33	Jane learns she is rich and promptly divides her fortune
34	Jane moves back to Moor House; St John wants her to go to India with him
35	Jane will not marry St John; she hears Rochester's voice calling her
36	Jane returns to Thornfield – learns about Bertha's death and Rochester's blindness
37	Rochester and Jane are reunited, and plan to marry
38	Conclusion

20	21	22	23	24	25	26	27	28	29	30	31	32	33	34	35	36	37	38	**Chapter**	
	●	●																	Gateshead	**Places**
																			Lowood School	
●	●	●	●	●	●	●	●									●			Thornfield Hall	
								●	●	●				●	●	●			Moor House	
											●	●	●	●					The School	
																	●	●	Ferndean	
●	●		●	●		●	●	●		●	●					●			Aspects of style	**Themes**
		●	●	●				●		●									Appearances	
		●	●					●	●	●						●			Bird	
								●	●										Books	
											●	●							Class	
	●				●		●					●			●				Dreams	
●		●	●	●	●			●		●	●	●				●			Environment	
	●							●	●				●						Fire	
	●	●						●											Food	
	●	●	●				●			●				●	●				Independence	
								●	●										Isolation	
	●	●	●	●									●	●	●				Love	
●	●		●	●	●			●	●		●	●	●		●	●	●		Nature	
	●		●												●				Passion	
								●		●				●	●	●			Stone	
	●	●	●		●														Supernatural	
				●															Adèle Varens	**Characters**
							●												Bertha Rochester	
																			Bessie Leavens	
																			Blanche Ingram	
								●	●	●									Diana/Mary Rivers	
	●	●																	Eliza Reed	
	●																		Georgiana Reed	
																			Grace Poole	
								●											Helen Burns	
●	●	●	●	●	●	●	●	●	●	●	●	●	●	●	●	●	●	●	Jane	
																			John Reed	
																			Miss Temple	
																			Mr Brocklehurst	
●																			Mr Mason	
●	●	●	●	●		●	●										●	●	Mr Rochester	
				●															Mrs Fairfax	
	●																		Mrs Reed	
								●	●	●	●	●	●	●	●		●	●	St John Rivers	
39	40	43	44	45	47	48	49	51	52	53	54	55	57	58	60	61	62	63	**Page in commentary on which chapter first appears**	

Commentary

Chapter 1

1 I was glad of it: . . .
Although we are unaware of the nature of her 'inferiority', look how quickly
Jane draws our attention to it. What does this say about the part it plays in
her mind?

0/16	Appearances
0/2	Jane

2 The said Eliza, John, and Georgiana . . .
Notice how Jane's isolated position in the Reed household is revealed in
these opening paragraphs. We are conscious of Mrs Reed's animosity but
also of Jane's ability to stand up for herself.

0/4	Isolation
1/3	Jane
0/7	Mrs Reed

3 Folds of scarlet drapery . . .
From her window seat Jane watches the rain and wind outside. The opening
paragraph of the book mentions 'clouds so sombre', 'rain so penetrating'.
What mood does the author convey?

0/30	Environment
2/4	Jane

4 I returned to my book – . . .
Books play an important part in *Jane Eyre*. In her solitude, Jane's imagination
is fired by the illustrations and writing of Bewick's *History of British Birds*.
Many of the illustrations were eerie and frightening. Why would they be so
fascinating to a young child?

0/5	Books
0/5	Dreams
2/7	Isolation
3/5	Jane

5 Each picture told a story; . . .
Bessie, the servant, was one of the few people who showed any concern for
Jane while she lived at Gateshead. She played a vital role in feeding her
imagination with tales taken from popular books of the 18th century. Jane is
reminded of these stories during the red-room incident when she describes
her image in the mirror as 'half fairy – half imp'. In Jane's unhappy position
in the Reed family what part did books play in improving her life a little?

4/21	Books
4/17	Dreams
0/11	Bessie
	Leavens
4/7	Jane

6 John Reed was a schoolboy of fourteen . . .
John is a most unattractive boy; notice how the authoress draws a parallel
between his physical description and his character. This is a common
technique also used to describe other characters in the book. Look at the
descriptions of Miss Temple in chapter 5 and of Blanche Ingram in chapter
17.

0/129	Blanche
	Ingram
0/7	John Reed
0/39	Miss Temple

7 John had not much affection . . .
Here is further evidence of Jane's isolation from the rest of the Reed
household. Not only does she have to endure John's constant bullying but
also the refusal of Mrs Reed and the servants to reprimand him. What must
be Mrs Reed's feelings towards Jane if she allows her son to behave in this
way?

4/9	Isolation
5/8	Jane
6/8	John Reed
2/18	Mrs Reed

	Characters and ideas previous/next comment

8 'Shew the book.'

One of the main themes of the novel is the striving for individual independence. Jane is constantly reminded of her dependent position in the Reed household. John discovers her reading Berwick's *History of British Birds,* one of the *family's* books, and does not lose this opportunity to emphasize her inferior place at Gateshead.

0/9	Independence
7/9	Jane
7/9	John Reed

9 'Wicked and cruel boy!' I said.

Jane's position is likened to that of a slave on several occasions. Look also at the next page. To call someone a 'slave-driver' at this time, would be more of an insult than nowadays, as slavery had only just been abolished. Why was Jane surprised by her own outburst? Notice how Jane reacts to John's assault. What does her fighting back tell us about her character? Notice that none of the household comes to her defence, thus ensuring her complete isolation.

8/10	Independence
7/19	Isolation
8/10	Jane
8/0	John Reed

Chapter 2

10 'Master! How is he my master?'

The position of the poor relation in a middle-class 19th-century family was difficult. Often he or she was given a home out of a sense of duty, not because of affection. In return he or she was at least expected to be grateful. You can see why, then, Jane's proud attitude was not well received. Even the servants were shocked by her behaviour. In their eyes her position was inferior to theirs because it was unearnt; look at Bessie's remark '. . . you are less than a servant . . .'.

0/23	Class
9/11	Independence
9/11	Jane

11 Bessie answered not; . . .

Once again the servants attempt to persuade Jane she does not know her place in the house. What qualities of character do they suggest she ought to adopt? Notice how they emphasize that it is her lack of money that makes her inferior. The connection between money and independence runs thoughout the book.

10/15	Independence
5/12	Bessie Leavens
10/13	Jane

12 'What we tell you, is for . . .'

Bessie, although always ready to support the family against Jane, is not unkind. Here she speaks to Jane 'in no harsh voice'. Miss Abbot, however, is not so sympathetic. What is the likely effect of her predictions on Jane at this point? Her lack of sympathy is noticeable, too, when Jane wants to get out of the red-room. Look at the description of the furniture in the room. What atmosphere is created by these colours?

11/20	Bessie Leavens

13 The red-room was a spare chamber, . . .

Notice Jane's sensitivity to atmosphere. The interestingly named red-room is described as 'chill', because there was no fire. Fire is frequently used as an image of warmth and comfort.

0/35	Fire
11/15	Jane

14 This room was chill, . . .
Charlotte Brontë creates an atmosphere of mystery and eeriness in the red-room. She builds upon the 'chill . . . silent . . . solemn' atmosphere, by telling us that this was the room where the uncle died. She also uses the image of the mirror to convey a sense of unreality, 'all looked colder . . .'. Even Jane's reflection reminded her more of a 'spirit' than of herself.

15 My head still ached and bled . . .
Powerful language is used to suggest Jane's tremendous sense of injustice, for example 'opprobrium', 'oppression', 'insurrection'.

11/19	Independence
0/32	Nature
13/16	Jane

16 I was a discord in Gateshead Hall; . . .
A strong theme in the book is the need to love and be loved. After much consideration Jane decides that her unhappiness is caused by an inability on her part to love the Reeds and for them to love her. If this was to happen there needed to be a harmony of personalities. In what ways does she suggest her character did not fit with theirs? Note the inclusion of beauty on this list.

1/25	Appearances
0/27	Love
15/17	Jane

17 A singular notion dawned upon me.
The power of Jane's imagination was hinted at in chapter 1, but now we see the full force of it. Trace the development of Jane's thought-process from where she ponders the idea of her own death by starvation. This leads her to reflect on her uncle's death and so to the idea of his spirit returning. Notice how the coincidence of this thought with a ghostly light shining on the wall triggers off terror in Jane's mind.

5/60	Dreams
14/77	Supernatural
16/19	Jane

18 'What is all this?'
Mrs Reed's behaviour proves Jane's point that her aunt was unable to love her. Jane's terror is interpreted as mere play-acting and Mrs Reed has no sympathy at all for her state of mind.

7/34	Mrs Reed

Chapter 3

19 I felt an inexpressible relief, . . .
Jane's inferior position is underlined by the arrival of Mr Lloyd, a mere apothecary (an actual doctor or physician would have been summoned for Mrs Reed's children.) Why do you think that Jane feels glad he is there? His departure has a strong effect on Jane. What words are used to describe Jane's feelings? Notice the image of 'darkness', used to describe her sorrow.

14/33	Aspects of style
15/24	Independence
9/26	Isolation
17/21	Jane

20 'Do you feel as if you . . .'
How has the episode of the red-room affected Bessie's feelings towards Jane? Is there evidence that she has more sympathy for her now? Look at her comment on Mrs Reed's treatment of Jane. Did she normally criticize her employer? However, she will always stand up for the family in front of outsiders. Look at chapter 3; why does she lie to Mr Lloyd?

12/28	Bessie Leavens

Characters and ideas
previous/next comment

21 Bessie had been down . . .
Jane's 'wretchedness of mind' after the red-room incident is shown in her attitude to the book she takes to read. Normally a source of comfort and imaginative delight, now the book mirrors her misery. Notice the words used 'eerie . . . dreary . . . gaunt . . . malevolent'.

5/36	Books
19/22	Jane

22 'Oh fie, Miss!' said Bessie.
Despite her misery, her deep pride cannot let false accusations go uncontested.

21/23	Jane

23 'None belonging to your father?'
Jane shows naïvety and ignorance of life in her response to Mr Lloyd's suggestions. Her experience of poverty is limited to her aunt's unflattering comments about her possible relatives and to the few poor people she has seen in the village. She has no notion of decent, working people. Jane's comment on the next page 'I was not heroic enough . . .' is indicative of the strict division between the social classes in the 19th century.

10/25	Class
22/24	Jane

24 Bessie invited him to walk into . . .
Notice the allusion to Guy Fawkes. What is he a symbol of? Note too, Jane's pride in describing herself in that way.

19/61	Independence
23/25	Jane

25 On that same occasion I learned, . . .
Class plays an important role in Jane's history. Had there not been the shame in those days of marrying 'beneath' oneself, Jane's mother would not have been disinherited and Jane would now have financial independence. Again, the emphasis is on Jane's lack of beauty and the implication that people would love her more if only she were not so plain!

16/33	Appearances
23/33	Class
24/26	Jane

Chapter 4

26 Eliza and Georgiana, evidently acting . . .
Jane's increased isolation after the red-room incident does nothing to lessen her self-esteem. In fact her utterance: 'They are not fit to associate with me.' shows just how strong it is.

19/43	Isolation
25/27	Jane

27 November, December, and . . .
The telling sentence 'Human beings must love something' underlines Jane's desire to love and be loved and it leads her to transfer her affection to her doll – for want of anything better.

16/45	Love
26/32	Jane

28 Long did the hours seem . . .
This is a good summary of Bessie's character, as seen through Jane's eyes. Jane acknowledges her kindliness whilst admitting her impatience and quick temper.

20/0	Bessie
	Leavens

	Characters and ideas	
	previous/next comment	

29 It was the fifteenth of January, . . .
Eliza is a mercenary character who was not above charging her mother interest on the money left in her care.

0/166	Eliza Reed

30 Georgiana sat on a high stool . . .
What is the weather like before Mr Brocklehurst's arrival? What does this tell you about the likely tone of the interview?

3/36	Environment

31 'Who could want me?' . . .
Notice the language used to describe Mr Brocklehurst – 'black pillar', 'carved mask', 'capital', 'stony stranger'. What do these words tell you about Jane's first impressions of the man?

0/234	Stone
0/47	Mr Brocklehurst

32 'What must you do to avoid it?'
Notice Jane's very logical answer to Mr Brocklehurst's question about avoiding hell. What would he have expected her to reply? Jane's approach to religion was not pious. Look at how she shocks Mr Brocklehurst with her comment on the psalms on the next page.

15/34	Nature
27/34	Jane

33 'I should wish her to be brought up . . .'
The role of Lowood, a charity school, is explained here. The pupils were to be made aware of their 'humble position', as poor members of the middle classes. How did their dress and appearance emphasize their inferior position?

19/38	Aspects of style
25/69	Appearances
25/49	Class

34 'I am not deceitful: if I were, . . .'
Jane cannot allow Mrs Reed to call her deceitful. Her sense of injustice is outraged and her anger and resentment cause her to speak her mind about her aunt. Notice Mrs Reed's reaction to Jane's outburst. To what extent does this scene explain Mrs Reed's deathbed summons in chapter 21?

32/44	Nature
32/35	Jane
18/171	Mrs Reed

35 I was left there alone – winner . . .
The imagery of fire here illustrates how Jane's sense of triumph soon turned sour. Whereas before we have seen fire used as a symbol of comfort and warmth, here it is used as a symbol of passion.

13/43	Fire
34/36	Jane

36 I would fain exercise . . .
Jane's shame and sense of desolation go uncomforted. She gains solace neither from the weather nor from her usual source, books. How does this explain her unusually demonstrative action towards Bessie? Notice how she describes the comfort she draws from Bessie: 'Even for me life had its gleams of sunshine.'

21/40	Books
30/37	Environment
35/37	Jane

Chapter 5

37 The afternoon came on wet . . .
We have already noticed how the weather in *Jane Eyre* is used as an indication of mood. What do the wind and rain suggest? Look back to

36/43	Environment
36/40	Jane

chapter 3 and to 'The moon was set, and it was very dark; . . .' on the last page.

38 The refectory was a great, . . .
Note the irony with which Jane describes the grace after this disgusting meal. Food is generally seen as a symbol of comfort and well-being in chapters 4, 7 and 8, but here it signifies quite the contrary.

33/47	Aspects of style
0/139	Food

39 I was still looking at them, . . .
The superintendent of the school is a kindly woman. Note her concern when Jane arrived at the school. Notice also her reaction to the burnt porridge episode on the next page. She is held in high esteem by the pupils, as can be seen in chapter 6.

6/47	Miss Temple

40 I read these words over . . .
Jane strikes up a conversation with an unknown girl, gaining courage to do so from a common interest – books. *Rasselas*, a book written by Dr Johnson, is a serious book suggesting that the best way to endure life is through patience and acceptance. Jane contrasts herself with Helen on the next page, 'I could not digest . . .'. What is the reading of this book meant to reveal of Helen's character? What does Jane's rejection of its offered loan tell us about her character?

36/140	Books
0/41	Helen Burns
37/41	Jane

41 The only marked event of the afternoon . . .
Notice how Jane reacts to the girl who is enduring her punishment passively. She is convinced that she herself would react differently and yet, when it is her turn, how does she behave? To what extent has Helen influenced her character?

40/42	Helen Burns
40/42	Jane

Chapter 6

42 In the course of the day . . .
The contrast in character between the two girls is very marked. Would Jane have reacted as Helen reacts to unfair treatment? Notice her telling remark, 'I wondered at . . .'.

41/44	Helen Burns
41/43	Jane

43 Probably, if I had lately . . .
Given her freedom-loving character, it is not surprising that this is her favourite time of day. What other factors add to her sense of well-being at this time? Notice how she wishes the weather was more violent, to match her exalted mood.

37/61	Environment
35/55	Fire
26/70	Isolation
42/44	Jane

44 'But that teacher, Miss Scatcherd, . . .'
Helen's attitude to punishment is contrary to everything in which Jane believes. How far are Jane's views based on instinct rather than thought? What role can you see Helen playing in Jane's life? Jane already seems susceptible to Helen's influence: 'I suspected that she might be right . . .'.

34/45	Nature
42/46	Helen Burns
43/45	Jane

45 I heard her with wonder: . . .
How far do Jane's views differ from the Christian view of 'love thy neighbour'? What are her views based on? Notice the importance of her words several paragraphs on: 'It is as natural as . . .'. Jane is susceptible to those who offer her friendship and love.

27/54	Love
44/46	Nature
44/46	Jane

46 'Heathens and savage tribes . . .'
Note the contrast in their attitudes. Helen accepts injustice with humility because of her deep religious belief that the wrong one receives on earth is of no significance when contemplating the eternal life of the spirit – 'injustice never crushes me too low . . .'.

45/48	Nature
44/52	Helen Burns
45/52	Jane

Chapter 7

47 'Your directions shall be . . .'
Why is Mr Brocklehurst's attitude quite unacceptable? Could bread and cheese be in any way described as 'habits of luxury and indulgence', or inedible porridge as a 'little accidental disappointment of the appetite'? His views are so extreme that their sincerity is in doubt – Miss Temple's reaction underlines this.

38/49	Aspects of style
39/50	Miss Temple
31/49	Mr Brocklehurst

48 Meantime, Mr Brocklehurst, . . .
Mr Brocklehurst discounts nature. He wants the pupils to be children of God. Charlotte Brontë emphasizes this contrast between the natural world and the world of strict religious orthodoxy. We notice this markedly with Jane and Helen in chapters 6 and 9.

46/52	Nature

49 'All these top-knots must be cut off.'
The hypocrisy of Brocklehurst's lecture is ironically shown with the arrival of his wife and daughters. Notice how little they conform to his mission to 'mortify . . . the lusts of the flesh'. He would not understand the irony, given his views on the education of poor middle-class children as revealed earlier, in chapter 4.

47/55	Aspects of style
33/136	Class
47/50	Mr Brocklehurst

50 The kind whisper went to my heart . . .
The public humiliation he imposes on Jane is further evidence of his cruelty and of the distance between his actual behaviour and professed Christian values. Contrast him with Miss Temple, who, as Jane said, encouraged the children 'by precept and example'.

47/55	Miss Temple
49/51	Mr Brocklehurst

51 Mr Brocklehurst resumed.
What does his description of Mrs Reed say about Mr Brocklehurst's own intelligence and sensitivity to people? Notice how, despite his biblical references and religious fervour, he metes out harsh punishment to Jane without proof of her wrong-doing.

50/53	Mr Brocklehurst

Characters and ideas previous/next comment

52 There was I, then, mounted aloft; . . .
Contrast Jane's reaction to the present injustice with the previous incident when she was wrongly accused. How does her behaviour differ? Who is responsible for this change?

48/54	Nature
46/54	Helen Burns
46/54	Jane

Chapter 8

53 'But what have I to do with millions?'
Jane's shame is lessened on hearing that Mr Brocklehurst is held in very low esteem. He is feared, but not liked.

51/56	Mr Brocklehurst

54 'No; I know I should think . . .'
Jane's desolation after her public humiliation is due to a fear that she will lose the love of those she holds dear at Lowood. Helen warns her that she thinks 'too much of the love of human beings . . .'. She encourages Jane to think beyond this life to God, and comforts her with the belief that God knows the truth about Jane. Although it is doubtful that Jane shares this view, Helen's words calm her.

45/59	Love
52/57	Nature
52/57	Helen Burns
52/58	Jane

55 Resting my head on Helen's shoulder, . . .
Notice how Miss Temple's arrival coincides with the moon shining through the window. Whereas darkness has previously meant despair and unhappiness (look at chapter 5) this light signifies hope and warmth in the person of Miss Temple. Contrast the warmth and cheerfulness of Miss Temple's room with the rest of the school. Look also at the earlier description of it in chapter 5. What does the description of her room add to our existing knowledge of Miss Temple's character? Again, fire is used as a symbol of comfort.

49/66	Aspects of style
43/72	Fire
50/56	Miss Temple

56 'I am afraid I shall never do that.'
The contrast between Miss Temple and Mr Brocklehurst is apparent yet again. Miss Temple judges others by their behaviour, not on their reputation. Her fairness of character is revealed in her willingness to discover the truth about Mr Brocklehurst's accusations. Look at the next page.

55/58	Miss Temple
53/65	Mr Brocklehurst

57 'How are you tonight, Helen?'
Notice the way we are carefully prepared for Helen's death. Previous remarks show Helen's readiness for such an event. Look at chapter 8, where there are several signs that she is ill.

54/59	Nature
54/58	Helen Burns

58 They conversed of things . . .
We have already noticed how Jane's behaviour is changing under Helen's influence. Jane's admiration for Helen increases when she listens to the learned conversation between Helen and Miss Temple. We are conscious that Helen has a maturity far greater than her years.

57/59	Helen Burns
54/59	Jane
56/66	Miss Temple

59 Next morning, Miss Scatcherd wrote . . .
Although Jane has taken heed of Helen's teaching on humility, she still cannot remain calm in the face of injustice. Note her indignation at Helen's treatment and the strength of the bond between them.

54/62	Love
57/63	Nature
58/62	Helen Burns
58/60	Jane

60 Thus relieved of a grievous load, . . .
Just as at Gateshead, so here, too, does imagination make life bearable for Jane. In what way do her imaginings show the truth of the final comment of the chapter?

17/81	Dreams
59/61	Jane

Chapter 9

61 April advanced to May: . . .
Consider Jane's response to the change in the season (look also at the previous page). Contrasts are also drawn between conditions inside Lowood and outside on this page. Charlotte Brontë makes use of this contrast for dramatic effect on many occasions, notably in chapter 26. For the first time in her life Jane has 'almost unlimited licence' to do as she wants, and this coincides with everything that gives her pleasure – the weather, sufficient food, plentiful conversation. Does she necessarily think that this is a good thing however? Notice the puritan streak in her which censures her own pleasure.

43/74	Environment
24/68	Independence
60/62	Jane

62 And where, meantime, was Helen Burns?
The notion of returning love for love is present in Jane's description of her feeling for Helen. Notice the words she uses to describe the way she feels towards Helen, 'strong, tender, and respectful'. Given Jane's passionate nature how deep are her feelings for Helen, do you think?

59/88	Love
59/63	Helen Burns
61/63	Jane

63 And then my mind made . . .
Why should Charlotte Brontë introduce Jane's thoughts on Heaven and Hell now? What is going to happen next? How different are the views of the two girls on this subject? (Look back to chapter 7, if you cannot remember.)

59/64	Nature
62/64	Helen Burns
62/64	Jane

64 'And shall I see you again, Helen, . . .'
Jane and Helen are totally contrasted in personalities and beliefs. The final example of this is their attitude to an afterlife. Helen's death is peaceful because for her Heaven is a certainty (hence her tombstone inscription 'Resurgam', which means 'I will arise'). Jane, whose sensitivity to the natural world is still so great, cannot think beyond the present.

Look at the last four lines in this chapter. Where did the marble tablet come from, do you think? This is a skilful use of the narrator technique by Brontë, who changes her time perspective as is appropriate to the story. Usually the application of this technique is quite obvious but there are many other occasions, as here, where it is done with considerable subtlety.

63/107	Nature
63/257	Helen Burns
63/66	Jane

Chapter 10

65 When the typhus fever had fulfilled . . .
Changes are made after the typhus epidemic and a management committee is formed to run Lowood. These men, who knew how to run the school properly and with compassion, draw attention to everything Mr Brocklehurst failed to be and do at Lowood.

66 I went to my window, opened it, and . . .
Miss Temple was more than just a teacher to Jane. Through her friendship and example Jane not only received an education but her personality was schooled too: 'I had imbibed . . .' says Jane. What causes her to revert to her natural self?

67 Here a bell, ringing the hour . . .
Jane is bored: she wants change. Freedom sounds exciting but she is practical enough to realize that she will have to settle for something less than complete freedom and independence.

68 'A new servitude! . . .'
Why does she *have* to settle for servitude? She is forced to be independent, to find a new situation herself. Notice her total lack of self-pity when she realizes this.

69 'Did she send you here, Bessie?'
Jane leaves Lowood, conscious of her lack of beauty; she still believes that physical appearance helps one to be liked. The scene with Bessie reveals how much Jane has grown up and been educated as a 'lady'. Bessie can vouch that her accomplishments are equal to those of the Reed children. What were the expected accomplishments of a 'lady'?

Chapter 11

70 Reader, though I look comfortably . . .
Jane experiences a mixture of feelings in contemplating her present state. What is the positive side of being alone, and the negative?

71 'Happen an hour and a half.'
Even if Mrs Fairfax turns out to be like Mrs Reed what does Jane feel is now different about her situation?

72 'Will you walk this way, ma'am,' . . .
Jane's welcome to Thornfield is warmer than she expected. Although Mrs Fairfax seems as Jane imagined, she was not anticipating such kindness. Notice the image of fire again, setting the background to Jane's sense of well-being.

Characters and ideas previous/next	comment
56/0	Mr Brocklehurst
55/69	Aspects of style
64/67	Jane
58/0	Miss Temple
66/68	Jane
61/71	Independence
67/69	Jane
66/85	Aspects of style
33/74	Appearances
68/70	Jane
43/231	Isolation
69/71	Jane
68/75	Independence
70/72	Jane
55/81	Fire
71/73	Jane
0/73	Mrs Fairfax

73 'I am so glad', she continued . . .
Jane takes to Mrs Fairfax because they both are looking for the same thing–company. Jane's limited acquaintance with kindness means that she does not take it for granted: hence her gratitude towards Mrs Fairfax. Notice also the other examples of home comforts.

72/74 Jane
72/207 Mrs Fairfax

74 The chamber looked such a bright . . .
The weather mirrors Jane's sense of optimism that life at Thornfield would, in the main, be 'pleasant'. Note the awareness of her lack of beauty again. Is this vanity, or a fear of putting people off? Notice also the importance of dress in creating an image of respectability.

69/92 Appearances
61/78 Environment
73/75 Jane

75 'I thought,' I continued, . . .
Mrs Fairfax's status as housekeeper and not owner pleases Jane. They are on equal terms and Jane is not dependent on her.

71/82 Independence
74/81 Jane

76 'Is Mr Rochester an exacting, fastidious . . .'
Mr Rochester's character is left vague but nevertheless our interest in him is aroused. Why does Charlotte Brontë introduce him beforehand in this way?

0/87 Mr Rochester

77 When we left the dining-room, . . .
A sense of mystery and possible supernatural activity is suggested by the upper storeys of Thornfield. How does this prepare us for the events that follow?

17/79 Supernatural

78 'On to the leads; will you come and see . . .'
The countryside around Thornfield is agreeable but unexceptional. Why do you think that Charlotte Brontë has chosen to place this description just here in the chapter?

74/84 Environment

79 While I paced softly on, the last sound . . .
The time of day and the ordinariness of the setting make Jane dismiss any unnatural explanation for the laughter she hears. The sight of Grace Poole, a very down-to-earth-looking person, makes her even more certain of a natural explanation.

77/86 Supernatural
0/83 Grace Poole

Chapter 12

80 The promise of a smooth career, . . .
Adèle's character is summed up rather cooly. She is average in her abilities, easily teachable, and the bond with Jane is not very close. Jane comments that her portrayal of Adèle is deliberately unenthusiastic. What is she trying to say about herself, while describing Adèle?

0/115 Adèle Varens

81 Anybody may blame me who likes, . . .
Jane expresses a dissatisfaction with present life. The education of Adèle and the company of Mrs Fairfax are not fulfilling enough. Her feelings tell her there are greater things to be had in life. Notice how we are being prepared for the arrival of Mr Rochester. We have noticed that when life is unsatisfactory Jane resorts to her imagination as a means of escape (as we saw in chapters 1 and 8.) Here again, in an attempt to come to terms with her growing restlessness and desire for more excitement, her imagination creates stories of 'life, fire, feeling'. Here, fire symbolizes passion.

60/97	Dreams
72/117	Fire
0/119	Passion
75/87	Jane

82 It is in vain to say human beings . . .
This is an important passage where Charlotte Brontë, through Jane, makes a plea for equality between men and women. In the 19th century more women were becoming aware of a lack of opportunity for them. Often it was a choice between governess or paid companion.

75/102   Independence

83 When thus alone, I not unfrequently . . .
Grace is a woman of few words and of unattractive appearance who, at times, likes a drink. Does she really sound like the kind of person who would let forth the terrible cries that Jane has heard? What are we supposed to think?

79/120   Grace Poole

84 The ground was hard, the air was still, . . .
Notice again how nature matches mood. The countryside which looks its best in summer and autumn is now bare and uninteresting. How does this compare with Jane's mood?

78/111   Environment

85 A rude noise broke on these . . .
Painting is used as an image to describe the disruption of the peace of the countryside. Later, Jane's use of a painting simile shows how she memorized Mr Rochester's face. Look back, also, to chapter 2. The important role art plays in her life is explored more fully in the next chapter.

69/96   Aspects of style

86 The din was on the causeway: . . .
Notice how Mr Rochester's arrival is linked to stories with a supernatural content – 'the Gytrash and goblins'. This element is present throughout Jane and Mr Rochester's courtship. What dimension does it give to the character of Rochester?

79/90   Supernatural

87 Something of daylight still lingered, . . .
Jane is conscious of his lack of beauty but already he strikes a favourable chord. Had he been handsome he would not have 'sympathy with anything' in her. In fact his 'frown and roughness' made her feel natural. Her concern for his well-being strikes him immediately as he notices her for the first time. This caring quality in Jane's nature is dominant in their relationship.

81/88	Jane
76/88	Mr Rochester

88 'I see,' he said, 'the mountain will never . . .'
The act of leaning on Jane is symbolic of their relationship. The words 'lean on me' recur again in the book (chapters 19 and 26) and symbolize their dependency on each other.

62/104	Love
87/89	Jane
87/89	Mr Rochester

Characters and ideas
previous/next comment

89 I did not like re-entering Thornfield.
Note how already Jane feels her 'monotonous life' is changed. Not only is she pleased to have made the acquaintance of a man but she is attracted by one so 'dark, strong and stern'. She does not look forward to returning to Thornfield, 'to stagnation', after the 'faint excitement' of her encounter.

88/91	Jane
88/91	Mr Rochester

90 I hastened to Mrs Fairfax's room: . . .
Note the significance of the dog's name. It was he who led Mr Rochester to Jane, and it is he who is the clue to Mr Rochester's identity when she arrives back at Thornfield.

86/94	Supernatural

Chapter 13

91 Adèle and I had now to vacate the library: . . .
The arrival of Mr Rochester brings change to the house. Why is Jane pleased?

89/93	Jane
89/93	Mr Rochester

92 'Is it necessary to change my frock?'
Having to choose the correct dress emphasizes the formality of the occasion, although by choosing the black and not the grey dress, what is Jane saying about the meeting?

74/99	Appearances

93 Two wax candles stood lighted . . .
A full description of Mr Rochester's face reveals a man who is striking but not handsome; he seems grim and angry looking. The lack of grace and polish in his manner (described on the next page) sets Jane at her ease. She is intrigued by him.

91/94	Jane
91/94	Mr Rochester

94 'Eight years! You must be tenacious of life.'
The sense of the supernatural, noticeable in their earlier meeting, is present again. Look at how Rochester teases Jane about belonging to the 'men in green', on the next page.

90/113	Supernatural
93/95	Jane
93/95	Mr Rochester

95 'For whom, sir?'
There is instant rapport between them. Jane understands the teasing, but Mrs Fairfax is puzzled.

94/96	Jane
94/96	Mr Rochester

96 I brought the portfolio from . . .
Mr Rochester's interest in Jane increases as he looks at her portfolio of paintings.

85/97	Aspects of style
95/99	Jane
95/98	Mr Rochester

97 While he is so occupied, . . .
Try to conjure up an image of these three pictures. They have a mysterious, wild quality about them. What do they say about Jane's subconscious mind, especially when we remember her comment that they are 'but a pale portrait'?

| 96/100 | Aspects of style |
| 81/119 | Dreams |

98 'I wish you all goodnight, now,' . . .
The mystery grows around Mr Rochester's character. His abrupt manner is explained partly by his nature, but also by some strange, unknown event in the past which causes him to suffer and find life at Thornfield unbearable.

| 96/99 | Mr Rochester |

Chapter 14

99 'Ah! By my word! there is . . .'
Mr Rochester is taken aback by Jane's frankness; but rather than take offence he uses it as an excuse to be as frank himself. Look at the next page.

92/117	Appearances
96/101	Jane
98/100	Mr Rochester

100 'You ought to have replied . . .'
Mr Rochester's comment is doubly ironic, when we remember how he is at the end of the book. Phrenology, or the study of the skull as a means of telling character, was popular in the 19th century. Hence Mr Rochester's reference to the 'prominences' of his head which were supposed to indicate conscience.

| 97/112 | Aspects of style |
| 99/101 | Mr Rochester |

101 'Now, ma'am, am I a fool?'
He is stung by her question as to his philanthropic nature. In the 19th century it was the mark of a gentleman to consider the poor and try to improve their social conditions. To be regarded as philanthropic was to be esteemed. Mr Rochester admits to being hardened by life but expresses a willingness to change. Who do you think will help bring about the 're-transformation from India-rubber'?

| 99/102 | Jane |
| 100/102 | Mr Rochester |

102 'You are dumb, Miss Eyre.'
Up to this point Mr Rochester has had total control of the situation. Mrs Fairfax and Adèle are behaving according to his orders but Jane refuses to submit to his wishes. Are his arguments for her doing so valid?

82/103	Independence
101/103	Jane
101/103	Mr Rochester

103 'Do as you please, sir.'
Notice the wisdom and pertness of Jane's reply 'your claim to superiority . . .'. What does this tell us about her ability to match up to Mr Rochester and the likely role she will play in their relationship?

102/104	Independence
102/104	Jane
102/104	Mr Rochester

	Characters and ideas *previous/next comment*	

104 I smiled: . . .
Jane is aware of Mr Rochester's consideration for her. Here, as always in her life, she responds to those who show her warmth. But although she feels independent enough to express her own opinion, she fully accepts her status.

103/145	Independence
88/117	Love
103/105	Jane
103/105	Mr Rochester

105 'And so may you,' I thought.
Notice how Mr Rochester's experience is contrasted with Jane's un-worldliness, in order to show his cynicism and her idealism. Mr Rochester has already referred to Jane twice as being 'nun-like' (look back to chapter 13). He envies the innocence that a sheltered life has left untarnished. What conclusion do we draw about his own life?

| 104/107 | Jane |
| 104/106 | Mr Rochester |

106 'How was your memory when . . .'
Mr Rochester talks with regret about his own lack of innocence and he blames circumstance. He feels he was born good but 'fate wronged me'. Our interest is aroused as to the nature of this unhappy event.

| 105/107 | Mr Rochester |

107 'Then you will degenerate . . .'
Jane takes on the role of moralist, criticizing his pursuit of pleasure and preaching reform and repentance. This is based more on common sense and an analysis of his own admissions than on self-righteousness. Look at how she becomes concerned for him on the next page.

64/108	Nature
105/108	Jane
106/108	Mr Rochester

108 'Distrust it, sir; . . .'
Rochester says 'You are not my conscience-keeper', but is that true? Is not part of her attractiveness to him based on his desire to lead a better life, to do what is right? Think of what he admires in her – her innocence, her unworldliness, her honesty, her consideration for him. Jane senses his desire for self-improvement.

107/113	Nature
107/109	Jane
107/109	Mr Rochester

109 'I am laying down good intentions, . . .'
In the conversation, which is 'all darkness' to Jane, we can hear echoes of future events: 'unheard-of combinations. . .', 'let it be right'. Do they not sound like the voice of Mr Rochester's conscience deciding to go ahead with a bigamous marriage?

| 108/110 | Jane |
| 108/112 | Mr Rochester |

110 'If you did, it would be . . .'
Jane is still reserved, cautious, and serious with Rochester; but he senses that she has a more vivacious nature that increased confidence will bring out. He uses the image of a bird to describe her character. Now it is locked in but on release it will open out its wings.

| 0/184 | Bird |
| 109/112 | Jane |

Chapter 15

111 'I liked bonbons too, in those days, . . .'
Notice the use of water as an image to describe passion at the end of this

| 84/140 | Environment |

long paragraph. Note also the contrast with the next paragraph which speaks of cold and steel.

112 We were ascending the avenue . . .

There is an element of the Gothic here in the dramatic description of Mr Rochester as he looks up towards the battlements. Look at the strong emotions in his face and the strong language used to describe his expression on the next page, 'wild', 'wrestle', 'pupil dilating', 'petrified his countenance'. What impact does this passage have on the reader? The suspense is extended when Jane thinks back to this incident and reflects on its meaning, in chapter 15.

100/120	Aspects of style
110/114	Jane
109/113	Mr Rochester

113 'During the moment I was silent, . . .'

Mr Rochester likens destiny to a witch, but he is determined to fly in its face. Again this is an echo of his attempt to marry Jane; already he sees her as the possible path to happiness and, more importantly, to 'goodness'.

The echo of the witches in *Macbeth* is ominous, for the central figure in that tragedy fell to his doom by trying to break the bonds of nature, order and justice; he, too, was met by those who spoke in prophetic riddles, like the 'hag' mentioned here. Can you identify any other figures in the novel who are echoes of this hag? Think carefully – there are two.

108/130	Nature
94/119	Supernatural
112/114	Mr Rochester

114 I almost expected a rebuff . . .

Mr Rochester is aware that this is not perhaps the kind of tale usually told to a young person in Jane's position. He points out that not only is Jane a good listener but she also has the strength of mind not to be corrupted by such stories. Notice again how Mr Rochester sees this as the source of his renewal. Look at the next page, when he says 'you may refresh me'.

112/115	Jane
113/116	Mr Rochester

115 'No: Adèle is not answerable . . .'

Jane's attitude to Adèle changes now that she knows the child is an orphan. Jane is more tolerant of her but still finds her character unsympathetic, particularly her 'superficiality', and is troubled that the child is not more liked by Mr Rochester.

80/126	Adèle Varens
114/116	Jane

116 It was not till after I had withdrawn . . .

Notice how Jane blossoms as she and Mr Rochester grow closer. He has become like 'a relation' now and she feels there is a mutual pleasure in the evenings spent together.

115/118	Jane
114/118	Rochester

117 And was Mr Rochester now ugly . . .

Ugliness is not seen where love is found: the personality shines through. Does Jane realize the same applies to herself? Notice the image of fire as comfort again.

99/121	Appearances
81/164	Fire
104/118	Love

118 And was Mr Rochester now ugly . . .

Although Jane is not blind to his faults (and she is able to list them) she sees them as temporary, caused by 'some cruel cross of fate', which, when resolved, will also dissolve the faults. Is this a realistic or a romantic view of love?

117/121	Love
116/119	Jane
116/119	Mr Rochester

119 He paused; gazed at me; . . .
The fire confirms Mr Rochester's suspicions that somehow Jane has been 'sent' to him. For the first time in his look Jane notices the presence of passion, 'Strange energy was in his voice . . .'. At crucial points in the book Jane has vivid dreams. The 'unquiet sea' of her passions is being kept in control by the 'wind' of reason. Why should she have that dream just then? What did the incident of the fire in Mr Rochester's room make them both aware of?

Chapter 16

120 I still stood absolutely dumbfoundered . . .
Jane's surprise to see Grace at all, let alone as unruffled as she is, leads her to question the possible reasons why Mr Rochester had not dismissed her. The mystery grows as we follow Jane's conjecture. She is not far from the truth when she asks 'What former caprice . . .'.

121 I hastened to drive from my mind . . .
Notice the change in Jane's appearance since her arrival at Thornfield. How far is this due to Mr Rochester's presence? Did Mr Rochester's departure that morning signify that he was afraid to stay and face Jane's questions?

122 Tall, fine bust, sloping shoulders; . . .
The account of Blanche Ingram brings Jane down to earth. Metaphorically, she puts herself on trial and judges herself to have been a complete fool to imagine that Mr Rochester could have any special feeling for her, a mere plain governess. She decides to take a tight rein on her feelings and to drive away any delusion about love. She makes herself draw her own portrait in chalk and Blanche's in oil and compares the two. Notice how the adjectives 'disconnected, poor, plain' in the title of Jane's portrait are the opposites of what were then considered eligible qualities for marriage.

Chapter 17

123 'You have nothing to do with . . .'
Jane's self-esteem is as strong as ever even if she has to adjust the focus of her feelings. She tells herself that it is undignified to show affection to someone who is not interested. Despite her will-power and self-control, look at how she reacts to the arrival of his letter. How well has she really schooled her feelings?

124 The party were expected to arrive . . .
Jane is still fascinated by Grace Poole. She is ignorant of the irony of her words when she describes her as 'companionless as a prisoner'.

122/125	Aspects of style
120/125	Grace Poole
123/125	Jane

125 The strangest thing of all was, . . .
The mystery surrounding Grace deepens as Jane hears half-stories of how highly paid Grace is for a difficult task. Her curiosity is aroused to find out the truth but she is sure she is purposely being kept in the dark.

124/128	Aspects of style
124/0	Grace Poole
124/127	Jane

126 It was with some trepidation . . .
Notice Adèle's excitement at having a house full of guests. She is absolutely delighted to be able to dress up and join the company; for her it is 'ecstasy'.

115/127	Adèle Varens

127 'What is it, Adèle?'
Jane is scornful of Adèle's love of dressing in fine clothes. Jane has always been aware that one creates an image by the way one dresses. Her preference for plain clothes (see chapters 11 and 13) is a way of saying that she is hiding nothing. Her personality is on full show. In contrast to Jane's simple clothes, notice the rich, fine clothes of Rochester's guests. The clothes, however, disguise the real people. Notice how they look like 'a flock of white plumy birds'.

121/128	Appearances
126/208	Adèle Varens
125/130	Jane

128 But the three most distinguished – . . .
Jane describes Mrs Ingram unfavourably and with a certain ironical tone. She stresses her haughtiness and pomposity. Notice again how dress is used to create an image.

125/129	Aspects of style
127/134	Appearances

129 As far as person went, she answered . . .
Remember that Jane is describing her and therefore her account will be biased. Admitting to her great beauty she stresses, though, that Blanche appears haughty and self-conscious. Note the ironical tone Jane uses to describe her.

128/134	Aspects of style
6/131	Blanche Ingram

130 Most true it is that . . .
This is the first time that Jane admits to herself that she loves Mr Rochester. Remember the early conversations between Jane and Rochester. Look back to chapters 3 and 14. How far do they confirm Jane's assertion that they have 'certain tastes and feelings . . .'? Notice her admission that to deny her love would be to deny her natural feelings.

121/136	Love
113/145	Nature
127/133	Jane
121/132	Mr Rochester

131 I feared – or should I say hoped? – . . .
Blanche's unpleasant character is revealed in her spiteful account of her treatment of governesses. Note the haughty way she dismisses them as 'nuisances'. There could not be a better subject to choose, though, to ensure the reader dislikes her!

129/132	Blanche Ingram

132 'Oh, I am so sick of the young men of . . .'
Blanche's views on marriage reveal her vanity and dominating nature, a
nature in which Mr Rochester is willing to indulge. Why?

131/135	Blanche Ingram
130/133	Mr Rochester

133 'How do you do?' he asked.
Rochester senses Jane's unhappiness and his concern for her is apparent.
Why does Charlotte Brontë include this brief meeting in the hall?

130/135	Jane
132/136	Mr Rochester

Chapter 18

134 'Will you play?' he asked.
The charades emphasize the play-acting aspect of these people's lives, just
as their dress and style of behaviour hide their true natures. Notice the irony
of Rochester and Blanche acting out a marriage. Is this not strange, if they
really did intend to marry? Bridewell was a prison in London. Where is the
irony here?

129/147	Aspects of style
128/137	Appearances

135 There was nothing to cool or banish . . .
By reversing the description of Blanche's character you have a description of
Jane's. All the virtues that Blanche lacks, Jane has. Why are they portrayed
as such opposites?

132/137	Blanche Ingram
133/136	Jane

136 I saw he was going to marry her, . . .
Jane senses that Rochester does not love Blanche and therefore concludes
that he is marrying for reasons quite common amongst his class in those
days, that is, 'rank and connections'.

49/138	Class
130/138	Love
135/137	Jane
133/139	Mr Rochester

137 Because, when she failed, I saw . . .
Jane senses that Blanche is play-acting in trying to win Mr Rochester's
affection. If she were not so self-centred she would realize that she was
failing. Ironically, Jane feels she could teach her a few lessons on how to win
his heart.

134/185	Appearances
135/0	Blanche Ingram
136/138	Jane

138 I have not yet said . . .
Jane has a very idealistic view of love and does not understand the 'marriage
of convenience' that was so common among upper-class people at that time.

136/274	Class
136/148	Love
137/142	Jane

139 But in other points, as well . . .
Note how she likens Mr Rochester's faults of harshness and sarcasm to salt and pepper which heighten the flavour of the dish – in this case, his personality.

| 38/164 | Food |
| 136/140 | Mr Rochester |

140 The want of his animating influence . . .
Note how Mr Rochester is the life and soul of the party. In his absence everything is dreary. Again the weather matches the mood. Note also the way reading is a symbol of cheerfulness.

40/251	Books
111/156	Environment
139/143	Mr Rochester

141 His manner was polite; . . .
We gain an unfavourable impression of Mr Mason. His face, though attractive, lacks force and intelligence. Inevitably Jane compares him with Mr Rochester and she is struck by the total contrast.

| 0/142 | Mr Mason |

142 Two or three of the gentlemen sat . . .
As if to confirm the immense difference Jane feels between herself and the other ladies, notice their totally opposite view of Mr Mason.

| 138/143 | Jane |
| 141/157 | Mr Mason |

Chapter 19

143 Mr Rochester has a right to enjoy . . .
Rochester understands her present feelings and sums them up perfectly.

| 142/144 | Jane |
| 140/145 | Mr Rochester |

144 'The eagerness of a listener . . .'
Her plain speaking and directness is uppermost throughout the whole interview with the gypsy. Look how she contradicts her here with, 'Your witch's skill . . .'.

| 143/145 | Jane |

145 'Your fortune is yet doubtful; . . .'
This could be Jane talking to herself after finding out about Bertha. The fact that Mr Rochester recognizes Jane's strong sense of independence and her deep-rooted integrity shows him the need to keep Bertha's identity a secret at all costs. Look carefully at this part of the novel – has Mr Rochester already decided to ask Jane to marry him? If so, what reasons does he give for not telling her the truth about his wife? Notice how Jane is not the only one who has resolved to keep her emotions in check. Mr Rochester, too, has decided to keep a rein on his. This is why he brings his ramblings to a rapid halt.

104/163	Independence
130/158	Nature
144/146	Jane
143/156	Mr Rochester

146 'Well, Jane, do you know me?'
Notice Jane's reaction when she discovers the true identity of the gypsy. Is it surprise mingled with irritation? Does she admit to being deceived? Why is she glad to learn she has been circumspect?

145/148   Jane

147 'The devil he did!'
Notice how Rochester's reaction to the news of the arrival of Mr Mason adds another element of mystery and suspense.

134/149   Aspects of style

148 'To comfort me?'
Jane declares herself willing to suffer the disapproval of other people in order to side with Mr Rochester. Why does she add that she would do this for any friend? Look also at the next page.

138/170   Love
146/158   Jane

Chapter 20

149 Good God! What a cry!
Notice the language used to describe the horrific cry and subsequent fear—'savage', 'sharp', 'paralysed'. Note too the exotic metaphor used to describe the cry.

147/150   Aspects of style

150 I saw a room I remembered . . .
The mystery increases. Jane is taken up to the attics and hears the noise again. It is very inhuman 'almost like a dog quarrelling'. She, of course, assumes it is Grace Poole. The suspense is prolonged as both Jane and Mr Mason are forbidden to speak to each other.

149/151   Aspects of style

151 I must keep to my post, however, . . .
The graphic description of Mr Mason's wounds is all part of the Gothic tradition. The atmosphere of mystery is increased by the flickering candlelight. Notice the use of such language as 'wild beast' and 'fiend'.

150/152   Aspects of style

152 And this man I bent over—. . .
The impact of Mason's arrival on Rochester is likened to the thunderbolt on the oak. Note the similarity of image at the end of chapter 23. How are the two connected?

151/153   Aspects of style

153 'Directly, sir; the shoulder is just . . .'
Note the Gothic image of vampires, and Mr Rochester's reaction of disgust.

152/154   Aspects of style

154 'That's well! Now, doctor, I shall . . .'
Again, note the touch of the exotic in the example of the mysterious bright red potion Mason is forced to drink.

153/155   Aspects of style

155 'The fresh air revives me, Fairfax.'
What is the connection between Mr Mason and the woman who savaged him? Why is he so concerned that he is reduced to tears? These are the questions we are left unable to answer.

154/172	Aspects of style

156 'It seems to me a splendid mansion, sir.'
Note the vivid contrast in language which describes the house and the garden. The house is 'slime', 'sordid'. Compare this to the list of sweet smelling flowers that are 'fresh' and 'fragrant' on the next page. Why does Mr Rochester feel this way about the house now? Why does he prefer the garden?

140/181	Environment
145/157	Mr Rochester

157 'Never fear – I will take . . .'
He describes his present life as like living on a volcano and he refers enigmatically to the damage that Mason might accidentally do him. (Of course it *is* Mason who does bring his happiness to an end in chapter 26.)

142/0	Mr Mason
156/158	Mr Rochester

158 'If I could do that, simpleton, . . .'
Mr Rochester knows exactly how Jane will react if she ever finds out about his wife (and he is right) and therefore he cannot even hint at the truth; hence the mystery that surrounds the events of the past night.

145/160	Nature
148/160	Jane
157/159	Mr Rochester

159 'Well, then, Jane, call to aid . . .'
Do you detect a self-pitying and self-excusing tone here? He wants Jane to condone what he has done – and what he is going to do. Notice how he refers to his marriage as 'an obstacle of custom', and 'a mere conventional impediment'. Is he trying to lessen its importance in order to proceed with his plan?

158/160	Mr Rochester

160 'Sir,' I answered, 'a wanderer's repose . . .'
Jane, perhaps suprisingly, tells him to look towards God for a solution. Does he not finish his answer because he thinks that he has found the solution in Jane? Mr Rochester is not yet sure of Jane's love, still less certain of his plan. Why does he prolong the pretence about himself and Blanche Ingram?

158/177	Nature
158/161	Jane
159/163	Mr Rochester

Chapter 21

161 Presentiments are strange things!
This first paragraph could easily be an explanation of the voices that send Jane back in search of Rochester in chapter 35. Notice how the rational side of Jane's nature tries to find reasons for the inexplicable. What do you think of her ideas?

119/183	Supernatural
160/163	Jane

162 When I was a little girl, . . .
Bessie explained that dreams about children are a sign of trouble. Look at the other time Jane dreams of a child in chapter 25. How does our fore-knowledge of the meaning of the dream help to heighten tension?

119/172	Dreams

163 'At all events you *will* come back: . . .'
Jane demonstrates her independence by only accepting the amount of money which is owed to her. She does not want more, despite Rochester's attempt to persuade her.

145/165	Independence
161/165	Jane
160/183	Mr Rochester

164 I reached the lodge at Gateshead . . .
Fire and food are again used as symbols of comfort. Bessie's kitchen had been the only source of comfort in Jane's cheerless life at Gateshead and now she is reliving this pleasurable scene. In what other ways were things still the same?

117/258	Fire
139/177	Food

165 In such conversation an hour was . . .
Jane feels she can face coming back because of her increased maturity and self-confidence. Which factors in her life have helped to heal the wounds and remove the resentment?

163/168	Independence
163/168	Jane

166 Two young ladies appeared before me; . . .
Jane draws a very severe picture of Eliza. Her clothes are very plain (although Jane should like this) but her face is unappealing. She uses such words as 'sallow', 'colourless' and 'ascetic' to describe her.

29/167	Eliza Reed

167 The other was as certainly Georgiana . . .
Georgiana is quite the contrast to her sister. Notice the words used to describe her, 'full-blown', 'languishing', 'blooming and luxuriant'. Jane does not, however, find her preferable. Notice how she describes her face – 'an indescribable hardness . . .'. The difference in their reactions to Jane is quite apparent. Eliza virtually ignores her while Georgiana views her critically and condescendingly.

166/174	Eliza Reed
0/173	Georgiana Reed

168 A sneer, however, whether covert . . .
Why was Jane so unaffected by the unfriendliness of the Reed girls? What has happened in the last few months to make their opinion of her quite unimportant?

165/169	Independence
165/169	Jane

169 'Mama dislikes being disturbed in . . .'
We see a more mature, wiser Jane here. She had always been sensitive to the unfriendliness of others, but now she is prepared to put up with the hostility of her cousins. She is learning to allow her reason to overcome her emotions. Why do you think Charlotte Brontë included this chapter in the book?

168/176	Independence
168/170	Jane

170 Well did I remember Mrs Reed's face, . . .
Again, notice the power of love. Jane's happiness, which comes through loving Rochester, breeds in her a new confidence and gives her a more charitable view of other people. Hence her ability to be unaffected by her cousins and, more so, to forgive her aunt, even to the extent of feeling pity for her.

148/186   Love
169/172   Jane

---

171 'A strange wish, Mrs Reed: . . .'
We can see on the previous page that Mrs Reed has not changed her opinion of Jane. Now we know the reason why she hated Jane from the beginning. Can we feel any pity for Mrs Reed when we realize her dislike of Jane was based on jealousy?

34/178   Mrs Reed

---

172 Provided with a case of pencils, . . .
Jane always uses her imaginative powers during passive, uneventful periods of her life. More recently in the novel we have seen her realizing her ideas through art (chapters 8 and 13). What does it say about Jane's present emotional state that she inevitably draws a portrait of Rochester?

155/188   Aspects of
              style
162/219   Dreams
170/178   Jane

---

173 'Is that a portrait of someone . . .'
Although Georgiana now deigns to talk and walk with Jane, what is the centre of their conversation?

167/175   Georgiana
              Reed

---

174 Eliza still spoke little: . . .
What impression do you get of Eliza's life? It is certainly busy, but is it meaningful? What does her obsession with routine say about her character? As a young girl she had a mercenary nature. Has she changed at all in this respect?

167/175   Eliza Reed

---

175 She told me one evening, . . .
Despite their contrasting characters they both share a total lack of feeling for their mother. Neither girl can wait until she is dead.

174/176   Eliza Reed
173/0   Georgiana
              Reed

---

176 'Georgiana, a more vain . . .'
Eliza admonishes her sister for her desire for company and frivolity. She exhorts her to do as she does: devise a daily routine which leaves one completely independent of all other people. In what ways does her idea of independence differ from Jane's? What very important factor does Eliza's idea of independence exclude?

169/182   Independence
175/180   Eliza Reed

---

177 True, generous feeling is made small . . .
The balance between nature and principle, or feeling and judgment as Jane calls it here, is one of the major themes of the novel. Jane likens feeling to a food that is too difficult to digest without judgment.

164/184   Food
160/180   Nature

---

178 Poor, suffering woman! . . .
Although guilt drove Mrs Reed to send for Jane, she is unable to reconcile herself to Jane and accept her readily offered forgiveness. What are Jane's feelings when her aunt dies?

172/179   Jane
171/0   Mrs Reed

Chapter 22

179 Mr Rochester had given me . . .
Although she does not enjoy what she has to do for Georgiana, she endures it. Note the wisdom in her decision not to complain, although there seems to be a certain self-satisfaction in her conduct.

178/180	Jane

180 One morning, she told me . . .
Why would it be contrary to Jane's personality to understand and agree wih a nun's way of life?

177/230	Nature
176/0	Eliza Reed
179/182	Jane

181 It was not a bright or splendid summer . . .
Notice how nature matches mood again. Notice also the symbolism of nature. The hay is being gathered in, the roses are out in the hedgerows. The time is just right for something, but what is it?

156/187	Environment

182 Well, he is not a ghost; yet . . .
Notice the inner struggle to control her emotions the moment she sets eyes on Mr Rochester. Charlotte Brontë uses the image of a veil to represent reason covering passion.

176/193	Independence
119/186	Passion
180/183	Jane

183 'Hillo!' he cries; . . .
Look at the language Mr Rochester uses. How does he describe Jane? What dimension does it add to their love that he should always see her in this 'other-worldly' way?

161/196	Supernatural
182/184	Jane
163/186	Mr Rochester

184 I knew there would be pleasure . . .
Jane adopts the bird image to describe herself. Mr Rochester previously also described her in this way. Here she is not a caged bird but a wild one, grateful to take the few bits of food (or comfort) that Mr Rochester has to offer.

110/192	Bird
177/256	Food
183/185	Jane

185 'It would be past the power . . .'
Jane is unwilling to express her true feeling aloud. Why? Notice the belief she has in the power of love to see beauty in ugliness. Is this a very romantic ideal?

137/193	Appearances
184/186	Jane

186 'Thank you, Mr Rochester, for your . . .'
The momentary triumph of feeling over judgment, which leads Jane to utter these words, marks an important point in the book. What impetus will they give to Mr Rochester? For the first time in her life she achieves her ideal; look at the sentence beginning 'This was very pleasant: . . .'. Her thoughts on what her feelings will be on returning home after an absence, earlier in this chapter, could not have had a happier conclusion. She is welcomed and feels loved by all at Thornfield.

170/194	Love
182/213	Passion
185/189	Jane
183/189	Mr Rochester

Chapter 23

	Characters and ideas previous/next comment	

187 A splendid Midsummer shone . . .
Notice the detailed description of the surroundings. Everything is perfect – the weather, the countryside in its fullness – the hay gathered in, the trees 'full leaved', the sunset beautiful. She even describes the garden as 'Eden-like' to underline the perfection of the scene. How is the author preparing us for the event to come?

181/198   Environment

188 I walked a while on the pavement; . . .
The scene is perfect. There is an air of expectancy. Something will happen. How does the cigar-smoke add to the air of suspense?

172/197   Aspects of style

189 I trode on an edging of turf . . .
His presence having been established by the cigar smoke, Jane attempts to avoid Mr Rochester. How does Mr Rochester's behaviour suggest the great rapport there is between them?

186/190   Jane
186/191   Mr Rochester

190 It is one of my faults, . . .
Through the description of the countryside, Charlotte Brontë has suggested the ripeness of nature. What is there to suggest here that Jane senses that the time is also ripe for her and Mr Rochester? How does this explain her reluctance to be with him tonight?

189/192   Jane

191 'Very soon, my – that is, Miss Eyre: . . .'
What do you think of Mr Rochester for falsely suggesting the Irish plan to Jane? Was there not a less cruel way to tear away the 'veil' from her feelings?

189/197   Mr Rochester

192 'Jane, do you hear that nightingale . . .'
What is the influence of the nightingale on Jane? Notice exactly the same effect a little later on. What would cause this reaction? Remember Jane's susceptibility to natural things.

184/195   Bird
190/193   Jane

193 'I grieve to leave Thornfield: . . .'
She summarizes what she has loved about Thornfield, and places special emphasis on the independence, intelligence and love. This is Jane's impassioned declaration of love. It is her continuing belief that beauty can influence love.

185/203   Appearances
182/194   Independence
192/194   Jane

194 'I tell you I must go!'
Consider the idealism behind her love. She claims it is based on equality, that it is a 'meeting of minds' not physical passion that draws them together. Is this true? Look at chapter 24 for evidence.

Notice how skilfully this paragraph mirrors the situation at the end of the book – when Jane will make what she says come true.

193/195   Independence
186/201   Love
193/195   Jane

195 'Jane, be still; don't struggle so, . . .'
Jane is likened to a bird again, struggling to be free. She reiterates her position of independence.

192/245   Bird
194/204   Independence
194/196   Jane

196 'Am I a liar in your eyes?'
Again he refers to Jane as being 'unearthly'; it seems to be always this quality which attracts him.

183/215	Supernatural
195/199	Jane

197 'Dear Edward!'
We are aware that Rochester still has something to fear. He is afraid of someone 'meddling', and he announces defiantly that he cares not what other people think. The mystery is, of course, about what. How does he question his own conscience? What good does he feel he is doing by now attempting to counterbalance the past misdeeds?

188/198	Aspects of style
191/199	Mr Rochester

198 But what had befallen the night?
What is the significance of the weather change? What does the storm symbolize, and how does this help to build up suspense?

197/199	Aspects of style
187/202	Environment

199 Before I left my bed . . .
What does the chestnut tree represent? How does it foretell the future for Jane and Mr Rochester?

198/200	Aspects of style
196/201	Jane
197/204	Mr Rochester

Chapter 24

200 While arranging my hair, . . .
Notice the use of the image of the mirror again. As in the red-room, the mirror is used to reflect Jane's perception of herself rather than the reality.

199/215	Aspects of style

201 I was not surprised, . . .
Love has given Jane new confidence. She feels that she is blossoming with happiness.

194/294	Love
199/203	Jane

202 I was not surprised, . . .
You could not get a clearer connection between surroundings and mood here. Jane is utterly conscious of the link: 'Nature must be gladsome when I was so happy.'

198/216	Environment

203 'Oh, sir!—never mind jewels! . . .'
Just as she dislikes elaborate clothes so, too, has she no use for adornments. To her they sound 'unnatural'. She rejects these along with fine dresses. Look also a little further on. She does not want to be an 'ape in a harlequin's jacket'. Can you explain her distaste for these things?

193/238	Appearances
201/204	Jane

204 'You shall sojourn at Paris, Rome, . . .'
He talks about being 'healed and cleansed' by Jane. What does this tell you about his view of Jane? Does it explain his use of 'fairy elf' and 'angel' to describe her? Think of the qualities in Jane by which he is attracted. Look back to chapters 13 and 14; 'I will be myself', she says – she makes it quite clear that she will not conform to any of the images Mr Rochester has of her, whether it is a 'court-lady', a fine 'beauty' or an 'angel'.

195/209	Independence
203/205	Jane
199/205	Mr Rochester

205 'I never met your likeness, Jane: . . .'
Mr Rochester talks about being 'influenced and conquered' by Jane. She teases him by alluding to Hercules and Samson, both of whom were ruined by falling under the spell of a woman.

204/206	Jane
204/206	Mr Rochester

206 He looked disturbed. 'What? . . .'
What question does Mr Rochester fear Jane will ask of him? Jane, however, admonishes him for his deceit about his 'intended' marriage to Miss Ingram. What is again noticeable about his motives for marrying Jane? What influence does he feel she will have on him?

205/209	Jane
205/211	Mr Rochester

207 'I feel so astonished,' she began, . . .
Mrs Fairfax is less than enthusiastic about the proposed marriage. Do you detect more than a note of motherly concern in her reaction to the news?

73/0	Mrs Fairfax

208 'Mademoiselle is a fairy,' . . .
Notice Adèle's lack of imagination and practical frame of mind in her replies to Mr Rochester's fantasy. She is very sceptical of his 'contes de fée' – his fairy stories.

127/0	Adèle Varens

209 The hour spent at Millcote . . .
Despite her love for Mr Rochester, she cannot bear him to lavish expensive gifts on her. Her pride cannot stand the feeling of dependence it brings. She likens Mr Rochester to a sultan and herself a slave. She loathes the thought of that status, and would rather he bought himself a 'seraglio' (a Turk's harem) than put herself in that position. The Turkish allusions are based on her reading of the *Arabian Nights*.

204/210	Independence
206/210	Jane

210 'I only want an easy mind, sir; . . .'
Notice how strongly Jane wishes to hold on to her independent position as governess, and to be self-sufficient on her wages. She wants nothing more from Mr Rochester than to be allowed to love him and to be loved herself.

209/212	Independence
209/211	Jane

211 'I want a smoke, Jane, or a pinch . . .'
Jane is determined to make sure she controls their relationship up to the time they marry. Notice Mr Rochester call her 'little tyrant'. Why is it so important to her that she makes her wishes clear?

210/212	Jane
206/213	Mr Rochester

212 He rose and came towards me, . . .
She is very calculating in her behaviour towards Mr Rochester. She makes it absolutely clear that she is separate from him; she is not like an Indian wife who would commit 'suttee' (that is, one who would kill herself on her husband's funeral pyre). Her honesty is so profound that she determines to

210/230	Independence
211/213	Jane

show Mr Rochester all the sides of her character, pleasant and unpleasant, before he marries her. There is no hypocrisy or deceit in her character. She is absolutely open and frank.

213 He fretted, pished, and pshawed.
Jane is so frightened of being dominated by Rochester that she keeps him at arm's length by deliberately being contrary and provocative. Is there not another motive too? She is aware of her physical passion for him and his for her. Is she not keeping this at bay too, by her prickly and unsentimental behaviour?

186/214	Passion
212/214	Jane
211/224	Mr Rochester

214 Yet after all my task was not . . .
Jane admits the full extent of her love for Rochester – to the point of idolatry. This is an important point to remember when we consider how she reacts after she finds out about his wife.

213/314	Passion
213/222	Jane

Chapter 25

215 The month of courtship had wasted: . . .
Look at the way Jane describes her wedding gown – 'white dream', 'ghostly shimmer'. How does this add to the sense of mystery and suspense in the story?

200/217	Aspects of style
196/322	Supernatural

216 I sought the orchard: . . .
The wind is a symbol of Jane's mental state. It matches the agitation in her mind.

202/217	Environment

217 It was not without a certain . . .
Look at the description of the tree. How far does it symbolize Jane and Mr Rochester after the news of his wife is broken? Notice how an uneasy atmosphere is created: the moon is 'blood-red'; it throws a 'dreary glance'; the wind lets out a 'wild, melancholy wail'.

215/218	Aspects of style
216/223	Environment

218 'Believe! What is the matter? – . . .'
Jane is highly agitated. She senses already that unhappiness might lie ahead. Notice how the suspense is building up again for the final shock.

217/219	Aspects of style

219 'No, no, sir; besides the delicacy . . .'
It has already been suggested that dreams about children forecast trouble. Again, the element of suspense is growing.

218/221	Aspects of style
172/220	Dreams

220 'I dreamt another dream, sir: . . .'
What connections are there between this dream and future events in the story?

219/250	Dreams

221 'All the preface, sir; the tale is yet . . .'
We are brought to the climax – we discover the cause of Jane's agitation. Notice the very Gothic language used to describe the apparition: 'fearful, ghostly, savage', 'bloodshot eyes', and also the mention of vampires.

219/224   Aspects of style

222 'It drew aside the window-curtain . . .'
When was the first time that Jane became 'insensible from terror'?

214/228   Jane

223 'And fasten the door securely . . .'
Mr Rochester draws Jane's attention to the change in the weather. Yet again it matches Jane's mood.

217/227   Environment

Chapter 26

224 At the churchyard wicket he stopped: . . .
Note the haste with which he makes his way to church. What are we meant to read into this?

221/225   Aspects of style

213/226   Mr Rochester

225 'Good-morrow, Mrs Poole!'
Note Brontë's use of language again – 'is this beast or human?', 'grovelled', 'growled', 'grizzled hair', 'wild as a mare', 'clothed hyena', 'shaggy locks'. How far is this an exaggerated caricature of a mad person?

224/242   Aspects of style

226 'That is *my wife*,' said he.
Listen to the bitter sarcastic tones when he says 'Such is the sole embrace . . .'. What is his attitude towards his situation – self-sacrifice or self-pity?

224/232   Mr Rochester

227 Jane Eyre, who had been an ardent, . . .
This is one of the most beautiful and poignant descriptions in the book. It echoes the previous description of the fullness of summer, which has suddenly withered. What do you think of it as a way of describing Jane's dashed hopes and numbed feelings?

223/229   Environment

228 Jane Eyre, who had been an ardent, . . .
Jane makes the decision to leave. Think carefully – what are her motives? She leaves not because it would be wrong to stay with Mr Rochester, but because he has betrayed her trust. Her initial feeling is that he cannot possibly have been sincere, he could not truly have loved her. In her moment of desolation, she turns towards God. Why is it a 'remembrance'? (Hint: look back to the text referred to around comment 214.)

222/230   Jane

229 My eyes were covered and closed: . . .
Charlotte Brontë uses the image of water to symbolize Jane drowning in sorrow. After an initial numbness she is completely overwhelmed by grief.

227/253   Environment

Chapter 27

		Characters and ideas
		previous/next comment

230 Some time in the afternoon . . .
Jane struggles with her conscience, which tells her that she alone must extricate herself from the situation. She cannot rely on the help of others. Look for example at the words 'you shall yourself . . .'. This is both an allusion to Mr Rochester's fate and a quotation from Matthew's Gospel.

212/244	Independence
180/237	Nature
228/231	Jane

231 I rose up suddenly, terror-struck . . .
She feels friendless; her sense of isolation, unexperienced for so long, returns in full – 'Friends always forget . . .'.

70/253	Isolation
230/232	Jane

232 Reader! – I forgave him at the moment, . . .
Her initial reason for leaving, given in chapter 26, vanishes on seeing him, and, although she still holds to the notion that she must leave, it will be so much harder now that she is sure of his love.

231/236	Jane
226/233	Mr Rochester

233 'If you think so, you must have . . .'
Mr Rochester is not surprised by Jane's behaviour. She is reacting exactly as he imagined she would. Notice, however, that unlike Jane, he has not yet considered the possibility that she might leave.

232/235	Mr Rochester

234 'Not in *your* sense of the word . . .'
Look at the phrase 'ice and rock'. This is a frequent image in the next section of the book. It suggests or describes a lack of emotion, the domination of reason over passion.

31/273	Stone

235 'Concealing the mad-woman's neighbourhood . . .'
Mr Rochester demonstrates that he was not heartless to his wife. What do you think of his behaviour towards Bertha?

233/236	Mr Rochester

236 'And take Adèle with you, sir,' . . .
Despite her weak state of emotional exhaustion, Jane manipulates Rochester throughout this scene, choosing her words and altering her behaviour to control his passion. She has always been the one with the firmer control of emotions and passion.

232/237	Jane
235/237	Mr Rochester

237 He bared his wrist, and offered . . .
Despite Mr Rochester's total refusal to accept the idea that Jane must leave, she still holds resolutely to her decision. Again, notice that she turns for support towards God.

230/247	Nature
236/238	Jane
236/238	Mr Rochester

238 'Well, Jane, being so, . . .'
Mr Rochester admits that he was taken in by outward appearances. He thought he loved his wife and, encouraged by the families who thought it was a 'good match', he married her. Is he not then to be held responsible for his own action? How far can it be argued that he was deceived? The qualities that Mr Rochester says his wife lacked are just those which he sees in Jane. How far does the contrast between his wife and Jane explain his initial attraction to Jane, do you think?

203/261	Appearances
0/239	Bertha Rochester
237/244	Jane
237/239	Mr Rochester

	Characters and ideas previous/next comment

239 'Jane, I will not trouble you . . .'

Mr Rochester discovered he disliked his wife and loathed her habits, described as both 'intemperate and unchaste', long before she was declared insane. Do you think he had the right, then, to disown her?

238/240	Bertha Rochester
238/241	Mr Rochester

240 'One night I had been awakened . . .'

If the treatment of Bertha seems callous, and Rochester's dismissive comment makes it seems so ('since the medical men . . .'), remember that in the 19th century psychiatry was very crude. People had not the same understanding of, or tolerance towards, mental illness as they have today.

239/242	Bertha Rochester

241 ' "Go," said Hope, "and live again . . ." '

He convinced himself of the rightness of his case. In his eyes he had no wife and so was free to look for another whom he could love ('a contrast to the fury . . .'). Look at the next page; do you think he was right?

239/243	Mr Rochester

242 'To England, then, I conveyed her; . . .'

Note the Gothic touch in the description of the prison: 'a wild beast's den', 'a goblin's cell'.

225/271	Aspects of style
240/0	Bertha Rochester

243 'Yet I could not live alone; . . .'

His account of his life during his ten years' wandering makes him sound very much a man of the world. He admits to keeping mistresses – that was a fully accepted situation for someone of his class – but he is eager to point out that he never indulged in debauchery.

241/244	Mr Rochester

244 'It was with me; and I did . . .'

If ever he thought he would be able to persuade Jane to come away with him then he has quashed all hope of that by his words 'hiring a mistress . . .'. Jane would never allow herself to be trapped in such a situation. Self-esteem aside, how does she consider Rochester would come to regard her if she did? Does Charlotte Brontë imply here that Jane and Mr Rochester are not yet ready for one another?

230/247	Independence
238/245	Jane
243/246	Mr Rochester

245 'On a frosty winter afternoon, . . .'

Rochester uses the image of a bird here to describe Jane's size.

195/252	Bird
244/246	Jane

246 'Impatiently I waited for evening, . . .'

Rochester admits he was attracted by Jane's wit and intelligence, and by the feeling of sympathy that quickly grew between the two of them. Look back to their early conversations in chapters 13 and 14 for evidence to support this.

There is an arrogance in Rochester's character that made him test Jane to see if indifference on his part would make her eager. In fact her conduct was always circumspect; she was always at pains not to reveal her feelings to him.

245/247	Jane
244/247	Mr Rochester

247 'Why are you silent, Jane?'
Jane's inner struggle is against, on the one hand, the claims of her feelings, and on the other, of her 'intolerable duty'. How far do you think she was rebelling against her nature when she did what she thought was right?

244/271	Independence
237/249	Nature
244/271	Jane
246/248	Mr Rochester

248 'It would to obey you.'
Consider whether Rochester is justified in using moral blackmail to persuade Jane to stay. What do you think of his question 'Then you condemn me to live wretched, . . .'?

247/249	Jane
247/327	Mr Rochester

249 Still indomitable was the reply –. . .
Jane is almost won over by his powerful argument. After all, she has no family, so whom would she be offending? But look at the integrity in her answer, 'I care for myself'. She has to do what she feels is right. Notice what she says about principles a little further on. Rochester sees Jane's determined spirit shine through her eyes and he knows that even if he could somehow force Jane to stay he would only possess 'the brittle frame'; her inner spirit would never be his if what he asked of her was wrong.

247/257	Nature
248/255	Jane

250 That night I never thought to sleep; . . .
Why does she dream of the red-room? In what sense is she experiencing the same feelings as she did then? (Look back to the beginning of chapter 27.)

220/283	Dreams

251 A mile off, beyond the fields, . . .
Jane likens her life to a book, the future being simply a blank page.

140/258	Books

252 I skirted fields, and hedges, . . .
It is Jane who uses the bird image here, 'birds were emblems of love'. To hear the birds sing hurt her for she is reminded of a deep sense of betrayal. She is betraying Rochester; is she also betraying her own nature?

245/254	Bird

Chapter 28

253 Whitcross is no town, . . .
Jane is set down in an isolated position, where no houses or people are in sight. Thus the descriptive background reflects her position – 'I have no relative . . .'. This imagery suggesting her closeness to nature is continued on the next page.

229/255	Environment
231/0	Isolation

254 My rest might have been blissful . . .
She likens her longing for Rochester to the feelings of a bird which is powerless to fly, yet still yearns to.

252/266	Bird

*Characters and ideas
previous/next comment*

255 What a still, hot, perfect day!
The rapport with nature that Jane referred to previously is now limited. As
Jane points out, she cannot survive on the fruits of nature alone. She is
reduced to begging. As if to emphasize nature's limitations she describes a
night quite different from the previous one.

253/269   Environment
249/257   Jane

256 I could not hope to get a lodging . . .
Food is again used to suggest a sense of comfort – but what a symbol of
Jane's destitution! Not even the pigs wanted the porridge, yet she 'devoured
it ravenously'.

184/262   Food

257 'My strength is quite failing me,' . . .
Unlike Helen who did 'submit passively' to death, Jane cannot. It is against
her instincts.

249/272   Nature
64/0   Helen Burns
255/258   Jane

258 Entering the gate and passing . . .
This scene must have epitomized Jane's ideal of comfort. The fire, the books,
the cultivated faces of the girls. Notice how strong a contrast it forms to
Jane's desolation and discomfort outside!

251/0   Books
164/260   Fire
257/261   Jane

259 I noted these objects cursorily . . .
What contrast do you see here between the Rivers' and the Reed's
households?

0/263   Diana and
           Mary Rivers

260 They withdrew. Very soon . . .
Recalling the image of fire is a skilful way of denoting Jane's sense of well-
being – and it is 'a genial fire at that'.

258/262   Fire

Chapter 29

261 On a chair by the bedside . . .
Always conscious of the effect of physical appearance on others, she is glad
that she is able to look respectable. Her pride had been battered by her
beggared state when she was taken in by the Rivers.

238/0   Appearances
258/263   Jane

262 It was full of the fragrance . . .
Notice again the two symbols of comfort used to express Jane's sense of
peace at Moor House.

260/292   Fire
256/0   Food

263 'That will do – I forgive you now.'
Jane has always responded to kindness. Here she is again amongst
sympathetic people and therefore their warmth brings her comfort.

259/266   Diana and
           Mary Rivers
261/267   Jane

264 Mr St John – sitting as still as . . .
This character has regular features, blue eyes and blond hair. Of whom is he the opposite?

0/265   St John
        Rivers

265 The three looked at me; . . .
Jane cannot 'read' his eyes in the way she could understand Rochester by looking into his. St John's eyes reveal nothing of his thoughts. They are only 'instruments to search' with. His curiosity leads him to insensitivity when questioning Jane. Notice her use of the words 'cold and stern'. Look out for images that reflect the coldness in his nature.

264/268   St John
          Rivers

266 'Indeed, you *shall* stay here,' . . .
Diana and Mary are both painted as very pleasant people, with Diana seeming the more open of the two. They have welcomed Jane and are willing to offer her a home. They are considerate and respect her privacy. They want to look after her as they would 'a half-frozen bird'.

254/328   Bird
263/267   Diana and
          Mary Rivers

Chapter 30

267 I liked to read what they liked . . .
Jane paints a picture of total harmony between herself and the Rivers girls. They share a mutual love of nature and of books and they share their different talents, with Jane being taught German while they learn about drawing.

266/0   Diana and
        Mary Rivers
263/269 Jane

268 No weather seemed to hinder him . . .
A conscientious clergyman, St John lets nothing stand in the way of his duty. Yet Jane feels he lacks the contentment that should have come from leading such a selfless life.

265/269   St John
          Rivers

269 But besides his frequent absences, . . .
Jane senses fairly early on that St John is very different from his sisters. For example, he does not share their love of nature or the sense of peace that a walk on the moors could bring. Jane senses that beneath his eloquent sermon lies a dissatisfied man who, like her, is still looking for a sense of fulfilment and peace of mind.

255/277   Environment
267/271   Jane
268/270   St John
          Rivers

270 'You need be in no hurry to hear,' . . .
St John himself suggests a restlessness of spirit – a feeling of not belonging here, of being 'an alien from his native country'. He awaits the call of God.

269/272   St John
          Rivers

271 'Do explain,' I urged, . . .
This explanation of St John's gives us an insight into how education was organized for the poor in the early 19th century. They had to rely on the benevolence of the richer members of the community. Notice Jane's reaction to the offer of the position of village schoolmistress. She does not regard it as having much prestige, but it offered her two things essential to her – shelter and independence. St John's attitude to this kind of job is interesting too. He suggests that Jane's talents will be wasted in this 'monotonous labour wholly void of stimulus'.

242/275	Aspects of style
247/293	Independence
269/275	Jane

272 'I was going to say, impassioned: . . .'
Again St John speaks of his restlessness, and he notices the irony in his own position. He, who preaches about contentment with one's lot, feels just the opposite. He sees the gulf between 'propensities and principles', or, in other words, between his 'inclinations and his beliefs'.

257/273	Nature
270/273	St John Rivers

273 Diana and Mary Rivers became . . .
St John's crushing of his natural feelings in favour of the demands of his ambitions is echoed by his sister Diana: 'He will sacrifice all' . . . she says. She thinks his decision is 'right' and 'noble' although she is saddened at the thought of his departure. Jane frequently uses the images of stone and marble to describe St John. Why do you think that she feels this is appropriate?

272/276	Nature
234/292	Stone
272/278	St John Rivers

Chapter 31

274 It is evening. I have dismissed, . . .
Do you detect in *Jane Eyre* a different attitude to class than there is today? At the time of the novel's writing there was still a belief that superiority of class also meant superiority of character. The egalitarian spirit was only beginning to become more prominent in society, with the feeling growing that people should have their character judged as it was found to be. Even the fairly open-minded Jane has to remind herself that 'native excellence, refinement, intelligence' are just as likely to exist in persons of one class as of another.

138/282	Class

275 Was I very gleeful, settled, . . .
Jane is doing this job entirely out of a sense of duty. She does not expect to gain much personal enjoyment from it. Does this seem strange to you? She observes her own feelings with her usual candour; she feels degraded because she has gone down in the world, although she has the sense to realize that getting to know the children might improve her liking for the job.

271/333	Aspects of style
271/276	Jane

276 Meantime, let me ask myself . . .
This is a very important passage because it sums up the major theme of this part of the book. Was Jane right to follow the moral code that her conscience dictated or should she have followed the inclinations of her nature? The

273/283	Nature
275/277	Jane

same dilemma is seen in St John's situation, and will be developed later. Already though, St John's sister suggests that he is ignoring his natural feelings by doing what he thinks is God's will, as we saw revealed in chapter 30.

277 While I looked, I thought myself . . .
She says that she has made the right choice, yet look at what happens! The close harmony between her surroundings and her nature denies this. She breaks down because her inner self knows she is not following her own instincts.

269/288   Environment
276/282   Jane

278 'Very well; I hope you feel . . .'
Notice St John's hardness of character when he sees Jane has been crying. She describes him as 'grave almost to displeasure'; he looks at her with 'austerity'. Would Rochester have reacted like this? Look how St John talks to Jane: he preaches and tells her how she should behave. He warns her about dwelling on her past life, about looking back like Lot's wife (whose curiosity for looking back on her city while it was being destroyed turned her into a pillar of salt). He pursues the theme of nature versus principle – 'It is hard work'.

273/279   St John
          Rivers

279 'A year ago, I was myself intensely . . .'
To illustrate his message that God's will must dominate over people's natural inclinations he relates his own experience: an ambitious man who was frustrated by the lowly work of a parson, he suffered for a year before he understood how God wanted him to do His will. He received the call to be a missionary. As you get to know St John's character better, consider whether it is possible to put another interpretation on his decision to become a missionary.

278/280   St John
          Rivers

280 'Good evening, Mr Rivers.'
Notice St John's reaction to Miss Oliver. First, he will not look at her (look at the previous page), then, when he does, he gazes without smiling. Yet Jane notices his inner reaction; he is moved by her, but holds himself tightly in control.

279/281   St John
          Rivers

281 'Not tonight, Miss Rosamond, . . .'
Only Jane could appreciate the effort of will it must have cost St John to refuse Miss Oliver. Jane had to admit he was as unyielding, as 'inexorable' as Diana had said. Why do you think he was like this though?

280/284   St John
          Rivers

Chapter 32

282 I felt I became a favourite . . .
Jane is happy to be warmly accepted in the village but she is very conscious of her social position. For her, 'To live amidst general regard' is important.

274/0   Class
277/286   Jane

283 I felt I became a favourite . . .
When has Jane always had memorable dreams in the past? Despite her superficial contentment (notice the polite and lukewarm vocabulary used to describe it – 'thankfulness', 'honourable', 'calm', 'useful') her true nature is troubled and restless. It is this that emerges in her dreams. For example, compare the kind of language which is used about the dreams ('agitating', 'exciting', 'force and fire') with that quoted above.

250/326   Dreams
276/284   Nature

284 Rosamond Oliver kept her word . . .
St John fights against his feelings for Miss Oliver, although he cannot prevent them showing on his face. Again, his decision is repeated: 'the heart is already laid on a sacred altar'. St John suppresses his feelings for Miss Oliver, not merely because his heart is dedicated to another cause, but also because his restless spirit would be cramped by domesticity.

283/290   Nature
281/285   St John
           Rivers

285 And then she would pout . . .
Miss Oliver is a very attractive character but do you think it likely that she would make a suitable wife for a missionary? Is St John right in feeling that it would be better for her to be married to someone else? If St John *is* right, what then does Rosamund Oliver see in St John, and is it the same thing which Jane can see?

284/286   St John
           Rivers

286 'Is this portrait like?'
Perplexed by St John's constant denial of his feelings for Miss Oliver, Jane determines to make him talk about it. He has not experienced her directness before and is surprised.

282/287   Jane
285/287   St John
           Rivers

287 'Does she like me?' he asked.
With more promptings she manages to break down St John's reserve and make him talk about Miss Rivers. He seems glad to do so. Notice how skilfully Brontë introduces the little detail of control: he takes out his watch to measure the time he allows himself to speak!

286/290   Jane
286/289   St John
           Rivers

288 'Don't imagine such hard things.'
Notice the use of water as a symbol of emotion flooding over a person.

277/327   Environment

289 'It is strange,' pursued he, . . .
Despite allowing herself the pleasure of indulging his feelings for Rosamond he believes that it is essentially 'delusion'. There is no place for her in his plan: 'Rosamond a missionary's wife? No!'

287/290   St John
           Rivers

290 'Relinquish! What! my vocation?'
St John sees his missionary plan as his means of salvation, 'his foundation laid on earth' as he calls it. Do his grandiose hopes of 'carrying knowledge' strike you as rather extravagant? Is St John just indulging his ego (or his 'self') with these grand ideas? Again, St John is surprised at Jane's direct manner, but she is 'at home in this sort of discourse'.

284/291   Nature
287/293   Jane
289/291   St John
           Rivers

How do Jane's conversations with St John compare with those she had with Rochester? With the latter, Jane was able to penetrate into and win 'a place by [his] heart's very hearthstone'. With St John her attempts to get to know him are foiled by his explanations. He refuses to admit what she sees to be the truth and accuses her of misinterpretation. St John insists that his blushes are ones of scorn and shame, not pity. He dismisses his feelings for Miss Oliver as 'fever of the flesh'; they do not come from the deep, from his soul. Jane does not believe him. Do you?

291 I smiled incredulously.

St John insists that he is driven by principle, not emotion, and he does show himself to be cold, hard, ambitious, and someone who cares only for his family – for whom he has what he calls 'natural affection'. Look how he regards Jane: 'a specimen of a diligent, orderly, energetic woman'! There is not much emotion there! St John believes that religion must shape all aspects of a person's life. Love, or 'natural affection', must be transformed into a dispassionate love for all mankind. He feels that his desire for power and leadership must be channelled into the life of a missionary, and that the job of religion is 'pruning and training nature'. How far is this attitude reminiscent of Jane's previous encounter with religion at Lowood School? How far do you think Jane agrees with these sentiments?

290/298	Nature
290/296	St John
	Rivers

Chapter 33

292 He sat down. I recalled . . .

Look at the description of St John's face as 'chiselled marble'. See how the metaphor stands out against the contrast of 'firelight'. What is fire a symbol of in this book?

262/0	Fire
273/300	Stone

293 Here was a new card turned up!

The money will bring her independence: that is Jane's reaction to the news of her inheritance. Notice how she seems to have little or no concern for the status or class advantage which such a large inheritance could bring her.

271/294	Independence
290/294	Jane

294 'Oh, I am glad! – I am glad!'

Which is Jane more delighted about – gaining a fortune or gaining a family?

293/304	Independence
201/312	Love
293/295	Jane

295 'Explain! What is there to explain?'

Jane wants to share her fortune four ways, for she feels that the money is not hers in 'justice', even if it is hers in 'law'. Are you surprised at this reaction of hers, knowing what you do about Jane? Notice her words to St John on the next page, beginning 'With me . . . it is fully . . .'.

294/297	Jane

296 'I think I can.'

What a cold fish St John seems! Look at the basis of his love for his sisters: it is 'respect for their worth'. His language is bland and unemotional.

291/298	St John
	Rivers

Chapter 34

	Characters and ideas previous/*next comment*

297 'Doubtless.'
Jane has a strong need for personal fulfilment. It is not enough for her to spend 'a life devoted to the task'. How typical is Jane of someone of her age in today's world? Would her attitude be considered as 'out of place' in a typical woman of today? Think carefully about your answer to this last question; ask yourself why you think your answer is right. Has the general view of a woman's 'place' in society changed much since the times of Jane Eyre?

295/299 Jane

298 St John smiled slightly: . . .
Like Helen Burns, St John urges Jane to look somewhere other than in this world for fulfilment. But Jane has always been very much one for finding 'the scene of fruition' in this world.

291/318 Nature
296/299 St John Rivers

299 'I mean, on the contrary, . . .'
St John's sense of righteousness is very overpowering. Look how he warns Jane about 'selfish calm and sensual comfort'. He reminds her that it is her duty to God to use her talents to the full; not to waste too much time on 'commonplace home pleasures'. Jane dismisses St John's preaching abruptly. She can judge for herself whether or not she is wasting her happiness on unworthy causes.

297/302 Jane
298/300 St John Rivers

300 Now, I did not like this, reader.
Jane sums up his character accurately. Note the images of stone again, 'his forehead, still and pale as a white stone'.

292/303 Stone
299/301 St John Rivers

301 'Tell him I will go.'
St John's uneasiness with domesticity is apparent. He is happier to be called out, even on the coldest night, because he can then consider his action one of duty.

300/302 St John Rivers

302 I found him a very patient, . . .
Jane is beginning to act according to St John's wishes. She already behaves in a certain way so as to avoid his disapproval and now she takes up 'Hindostanee', not because she wanted to, but because he was 'not a man to be lightly refused'. His hold on her grows as she modifies her behaviour more and more, according to his approval and disapproval. How different from the way she behaved with Mr Rochester!

299/303 Jane
301/303 St John Rivers

303 I found him a very patient, . . .
Notice the image of cold again. She talks of coming under a 'freezing spell'. In what way is her personality frozen? What tells you that she will eventually react to this new 'servitude'?

300/316 Stone
302/304 Jane
300/316 St John Rivers

304 She pushed me towards him.
Look how she analyses her nightly kiss. The kiss is given by St John more to see how she would react than because of any sentiment of his own. The kiss seems to Jane to lock her into slavery, 'a seal affixed to my fetters', as she says. An important point about the relationship between Jane and St John is

294/309 Independence
303/305 Jane
303/305 St John Rivers

that she has to suppress half of her personality and follow pursuits that she does not care for. He is moulding her and she does not like it.

305 St John called me to his side . . .

How unlike herself she has become! Her natural spirits have been so strong and have always fought back; they were thriving at Thornfield, but are now very low. She has not the strength to stand up to St John, but complies with every decision he makes about how she should be occupying herself. Note his total detachment as he watches Jane cry; there is no sympathy, no comfort. He is just 'like a physician watching with the eye of science'.

304/306	Jane
304/307	St John Rivers

306 I know no medium: . . .

Jane explains why she is behaving in this uncharacteristic way. Why is it, do you think, that she is not yet ready to revolt?

305/308	Jane

307 'Yes,' said he, 'there is my glory . . .'

Notice St John's attitude – he assumes that he is above other men, directed and controlled solely by God.

305/308	St John Rivers

308 'And what does *your* heart say?'

How different this is from Rochester's proposal! For St John it was solely a marriage of convenience, based on his notion that Jane would be a hard worker, she being 'formed for labour, not for love'. To what extent do you think he knows Jane's true character?

306/309	Jane
307/311	St John Rivers

309 'But my powers – where are they . . .'

Jane has always relied on her instincts to determine whether something is right or wrong. She now explains that they are not responding, not telling her that this is the correct path to follow. Her use of 'fettered' helps to reinforce this feeling of hers to the reader. She feels she is being chained, 'enslaved' again.

304/313	Independence
308/310	Jane

310 'I have an answer for you – hear it.'

How many of these characteristics belong to the real Jane? How many of them are assumed in order simply to please St John?

309/311	Jane

311 'I am ready to go to India, . . .'

Reread Jane's reasoning up to this point. Why do you think she is prepared to go with St John? However, what particular notion does she reject which finally makes her say no?

310/312	Jane
308/312	St John Rivers

312 'And I will give the missionary . . .'

A marriage without love would be a pretence and for that reason she can only go to India as his sister, not his wife. What caused Jane to shudder? What is it about St John's attitude to a wife that is so abhorrent to her? It is St John's arrogance when saying 'I cannot accept on His behalf' that makes Jane aware that he, too, has faults. Her natural wit is aroused and she answers him sarcastically.

294/314	Love
294/314	Jane
311/313	St John Rivers

313 I will not swear, reader, . . .
This is an important moment for Jane. She sees St John as a human being, with faults as well as virtues. Now she can begin to have confidence, to be herself again. The spell she was under is broken: notice how she asserts 'I was with an equal'. As she says a little further on, she is now able to discriminate between 'the Christian' and the man.

309/0	Independence
312/314	Jane
312/315	St John
	Rivers

314 'Shall I?' I said, briefly; . . .
She considers the situation again. She knows she could endure being his companion because there would be distance enough between them for her to still feel free in 'heart and mind'. But she could not marry without love; she could not be 'forced to keep the fire of my nature continually low'. Notice the vehemence with which she addresses St John. Her old forthrightness has returned and her grip over her true nature is firm again.

312/316	Love
214/0	Passion
313/316	Jane

315 'Then shake hands,' I added.
Jane was able to distinguish 'the Christian from the man' and whilst she had not felt able to resist the demands of the Christian, this gave her the courage to stand up to the man. In the last scene of this chapter the same distinction is made. The man in St John is offended and refuses to say goodnight, but the Christian suffers the blow to his pride silently and patiently, although at the end it is the man who pretends it is otherwise.

313/316	St John
	Rivers

Chapter 35

316 He did not abstain from conversing . . .
Interestingly, and importantly, St John does not represent the Christian notion of forgiveness. He says he has forgiven Jane, but he cannot forget, and this shows in his behaviour towards her: he is as cold and hard as marble. From what we have learnt about Jane's character it seems very clear that this lack of warmth would stifle her spirit. She could not live with someone who showed no pity (like Ruth), and who had no inclination to repair the gap which had opened between them.

314/0	Love
303/0	Stone
314/319	Jane
315/317	St John
	Rivers

317 'St John, I am unhappy, . . .'
This sums up St John's attitude to life and religion. He is so dominated by principle that he lacks compassion.

316/318	St John
	Rivers

318 His lips and cheeks turned white−. . .
Notice again St John's lack of sympathy and the domination of religious teaching in his thinking. He quotes the Gospel well enough, yet he does not carry it out. By his behaviour he shows he has not forgiven Jane. Consider why he is so offended by her words which he calls 'violent, unfeminine, untrue'. What is the reason for this struggle in him between Nature and Grace, between emotion and principle? What natural feelings is he having to try to conquer now? (Hint: look forward a couple of paragraphs to 'A fresh wrong did . . . '.)

298/319	Nature
317/319	St John
	Rivers

319 'A female curate, who is not . . .'
Notice again St John's rigid adherence to rules and principles. He tries to make Jane feel guilty by talking about 'the dishonour' of her breaking her promise to him! Fortunately for Jane, she now has a clearer view of his character and can put what he says into a wider perspective – she is therefore more sure of her own position and can answer without fear and without guilt. The two characters are totally contrasted; he is motivated by religious principle, she by natural 'common sense'. He believes in the good of sacrifice; she sees no point in it ('God did not give men . . .'). Her instinct for survival is one of her most pronounced characteristics, one which saw her through all the difficult phases of her life – a life that she is not going to give up easily. Look what other strong force compels her to stay in Britain. St John is aware of the importance of Rochester – he describes their love as 'lawless and unconsecrated'. What does this tell you about the way he sees everything?

318/323	Nature
316/320	Jane
318/320	St John Rivers

320 'And yet, St John is a good man,' . . .
Jane sums up his character well, and she sums up why she feels she could not live with him. She has already experienced 'the trampling' of her personality.

319/321	Jane
319/321	St John Rivers

321 'Could you decide now?'
It is only when she can see the man behind the priest that she can be herself and stand up to St John. Notice how she succumbs to his influence once more.

320/322	Jane
320/322	St John Rivers

322 'I could decide if I were but certain,' . . .
It is important to be clear about what Jane has agreed to here. She succumbs in so far as she says she will submit to *God's* will – not St John's. She is desperate to do the right thing but look at how her judgment is unclear ('I contended with my inward . . .'). Is the voice of Mr Rochester, as an echo of her own nature, answering her plea for guidance?

321/323	Jane
321/330	St John Rivers
215/323	Supernatural

323 All the house was still; . . .
Jane's closeness to nature has been seen throughout the book. Her moods have been both susceptible to and mirrored by those of nature, and she gives herself up to it on leaving Thornfield. (Remember, though, that this is actually a skilled piece of writing on Brontë's part in her use of the previously explained 'pathetic fallacy'. See 'Environment' on page 10.)

Jane's sense of God and of the supernatural are both linked to nature; her feelings of right and wrong are based on what she feels is 'natural'. It is only now that she has fully worked this out; she has had to reject the laws that have been taught to her in the name of religion. She has found her own God now ('I seemed to penetrate . . .') and she knows what it is right for her to do.

319/324	Nature
322/324	Jane
322/0	Supernatural

Chapter 36

324 'My spirit,' I answered, . . .
Jane is still considering exactly how to do what is right but feels that she is now facing in the correct direction. She is ready to 'search – enquire . . .', not

323/0	Nature
323/325	Jane

just for Mr Rochester but also for truth. Do you feel that she thinks the two are linked?

---

325 It was the first of June; . . .
She feels the voice, whether it was real or imagined, has had a liberating effect on her mind. It showed her the right path to follow.

324/326   Jane

---

326 'Yes, ma'am! I lived there once.'
Jane's dreams have come true. Look back to chapter 25 to see what she dreamt about, and notice how that chapter exactly parallels this one.

328/0   Dreams
325/329   Jane

Chapter 37

327 To this house I came, . . .
Notice the weather when Jane arrives at Ferndean. Whose mood does it coincide with? Notice also the location of Ferndean, hidden away and surrounded by dark woods. What does this suggest to you about Rochester's state of mind? Look carefully at Brontë's use of the elements – the weather changes the next day, along with Rochester's mood – 'The rain is over and gone . . .'.

288/0   Environment
248/328   Mr
           Rochester

---

328 I stayed my step, almost my breath, . . .
It is usually Jane who is described as a bird but here Charlotte Brontë uses this image to illustrate Mr Rochester's unhappiness at being chained to Ferndean. Notice how the imagery is pursued about four pages on. Do you think an 'eagle' is a fitting image for Mr Rochester?

266/332   Bird
327/329   Mr
           Rochester

---

329 'Which I never will, sir, . . .'
Already we can detect a change in their relationship. She would never before have been the first to make her intentions clear. Notice also the lighthearted tone in which she speaks.

326/330   Jane
328/330   Mr
           Rochester

---

330 He replied not: he seemed serious – . . .
Why does Mr Rochester think that she will not want to marry him now? She draws a contrast between the way she had to behave with St John and the way she behaves now with Mr Rochester. She is now at 'perfect ease', her 'whole nature' has been 'brought to life and light'. That is her idea of love.

329/331   Jane
329/331   Mr
           Rochester
322/331   St John
           Rivers

---

331 'Have you a pocket-comb about you, . . .'
Jane's relationship with Rochester – the ease, the rapport, the knowing how to please, the teasing – is in complete contrast to the relationship between St John and Jane! Look at how natural with each other Jane and Rochester seem.

330/332   Jane
330/332   Mr
           Rochester
330/335   St John
           Rivers

---

332 'It is a bright, sunny morning, sir,' . . .
Bird imagery is used to describe both of them. The pleasure of hearing her
voice makes Rochester liken her to a skylark. He is still the chained 'eagle'
dependent now on a mere 'sparrow'. Why is this note of dependence, new
to their relationship, so important?

328/0	Bird
331/333	Jane
331/333	Mr Rochester

333 'I am no better than . . .'
Notice the reference to the old chestnut tree. This image of plants growing in
the shelter of the tree is a beautiful description of her love for Mr Rochester.

275/0	Aspects of style
332/0	Jane
332/334	Mr Rochester

334 He pursued his own thoughts . . .
Notice the comment that 'Divine justice pursued its course'. Rochester
begins to see the workings of God behind his sad fate. In what ways is he a
better man for his deformities? What personality traits has it affected and
how does it put him on a more equal footing with Jane? Consider your own
views about the appropriateness of this kind of divine retribution.

333/335	Mr Rochester

Chapter 38

335 As to St John Rivers, . . .
St John is still soldiering on in India, converting the natives, clearing 'their
painful way to improvement', while at the same time ensuring himself 'a
place in the first rank . . .'. Notice the contrast between the approach of St
John to God, and Mr Rochester's humble approach. Rochester's road is one
of humility through misfortune, of salvation through the goodness of love.
Think about which of these two opposing approaches would be most
supported by Charlotte Brontë.

334/0	Mr Rochester
331/0	St John Rivers

Characters in the novel

This is a very brief overview of each character. You should use it as a starting point for your own studies of characterization. For each of the aspects of character mentioned you should look in your text for evidence to support or contradict the views expressed here, and indeed, your own views as well.

Know the incidents and conversations which will support and enlarge upon your knowledge of each character. You will find it helpful to select a character and follow the commentary, referring always to the text to read and digest the context of the comment.

Adèle Varens

She is a very lively but rather frivolous young girl who loves clothes, dancing and presents. She is not very studious or imaginative but Jane finds her pliable and obedient. She is under the protection of Mr Rochester, following her disputed parenthood, and her background is involved with his previous wild life in Europe.

Bertha Rochester

Charlotte Brontë paints a picture of Bertha Rochester which is so layered with Gothic overtones that it is difficult to get at the real personality. The manic side of her nature is stressed, as is her violence, her screams, and her black, tangled hair. According to Mr Rochester she was a handsome figure before her insanity set in, even if she was not very imaginative or intelligent. It is she who is responsible for the destruction of the suggestively named Thornfield Hall.

Bessie Leavens

Bessie, the nursemaid at Gateshead, is the only person who has any liking for Jane. Although careful not to contradict the wishes of her mistress, she does show kindness to Jane and gives her small treats for comfort when she can. She has a quick temper and is not slow to admonish Jane if necessary. She is cheerful and has a store of tales with which she entertains the children.

Blanche Ingram

She is very handsome woman, well dressed and highly accomplished in the expected pursuits of a lady. She is very self-centred and haughty towards others. She finds Adèle irritating and treats Jane, as a mere governess, very scornfully. Her attempts at courtship with Mr Rochester are simply a pretence, for it transpires that she is interested only in the money and social position that marrying him would bring.

Diana and Mary Rivers

Both sisters are friendly, pleasant, interested in learning, and have loving natures towards Jane and their brother. They are the antithesis of the Reed sisters. Diana is the more dominant of the two, and Jane holds her in particular affection.

Eliza Reed

Eliza is a mercenary, calculating child who grows into a narrow-minded, puritanical woman. She has no time for other people (she does not speak to Jane or mourn her mother). She is totally engrossed in the rituals of religion. Her day is strictly divided into routine activities, which are carried out faithfully every day. On the death of her mother, she leaves to become a nun. In many ways she is the female counterpart of St John Rivers.

Georgiana Reed

Georgiana is the absolute opposite of her sister. Fair, where her sister is dark, she is concerned only about her appearance and her social life. Each of the sisters is totally self-centred in their own way. Neither of them care for their mother and both use Jane to further their own ends. Georgiana is somewhat like Blanche Ingram.

Grace Poole

Grace is a plain, steady but uncommunicative woman. It is difficult for Jane to imagine that Grace could be responsible for the maniacal cries that are heard from time to time at Thornfield. She does her job as Bertha's guardian efficiently except on the occasions when she succumbs to her weakness for drink. It is during these lapses that Mrs Rochester is able to get out and do her damage.

Helen Burns

Helen Burns is the epitome of goodness. She demonstrates the doctrine of Christian tolerance to the full. She is patient, long suffering and very ready to admit her faults. She endures punishment for her inattentiveness and untidiness without complaint. She is serious, studious, and very philosophical about injustice. Helen acts as a foil to Jane's passionate, untrained nature which, thanks to her influence, is somewhat schooled. She faces death with calmness and equanimity, sure in the knowledge of an afterlife.

Jane Eyre

Jane is small and plain, facts which shape her character and behaviour. She believes it is for these reasons that she is unloved and this encourages her to develop her wit and pertness as ways of becoming noticed. She is endowed with a strong, passionate temperament, which leads her into trouble at Gateshead. At Lowood she learns to control her feelings, but they remain always ready to burst forth. This they do under the guise of adult love at Thornfield, but yet again she is forced to rein them. Only at Moor House does she fully come to terms with her feelings and her nature, and this enables her to indulge them freely in their true place at Ferndean. She is an intelligent, plain-speaking person, who shows herself to be principled and strong-willed.

John Reed

As a child John Reed is utterly spoilt by his mother. He is greedy and a bully and he makes life very hard for Jane. The weakness in his character leads him into bad company as an adult. Later in the novel we learn that he has caused his mother much expense and heartbreak before he finally commits suicide.

Miss Temple

Miss Temple is a gracious, fair-minded lady who treats the girls at Lowood with respect and justice. She resolves the question of Jane's public disgrace by finding out the truth from Mr Lloyd. She orders extra food when the cooking is bad. She is admired because she practices what she preaches, unlike Mr Brocklehurst. She has a particular affection for Helen, whom she knows is dying. She is the biggest influence on Jane during the eight years she is at Lowood School.

Mr Brocklehurst

Mr Brocklehurst is a tall, grim-faced man who imposes a harsh discipline on Lowood School. He is strict to the point of cruelty and unloved by the pupils. His religious teaching dwells not on Christian love and tolerance, but on sin and domination. He is a hypocrite who lives in comfort with his family whilst the pupils at Lowood freeze and starve because he feels that it is good for their souls.

Mr Mason

Mr Mason is a handsome but weak man, whom Jane dislikes from the start. He has an affection for his mad sister, Bertha Rochester, though he is frightened of Mr Rochester. It is he who causes the wedding to be stopped.

Mr Rochester

Mr Rochester is attractive but not handsome; he is dark and strong. He is lively, loves company, and is witty but also arrogant. A man of the world, he is much given to moods, and there is an air of mystery about him. He reveals himself to be very loving and passionate but also tolerant and not overbearing. He is seeking after goodness (which he finds in Jane) and only after a struggle does he elect to do the unlawful act of attempting to marry Jane whilst his wife Bertha is still alive. His treatment of Bertha shows compassion although he is self-pitying in his attitude to his fate. During the events surrounding the destruction of Thornfield and the death of Bertha he is humbled by the loss of eye and limb, which leaves him able to build a more equal relationship with Jane when she returns to him.

Mrs Fairfax

Mrs Fairfax is the very efficient housekeeper of Thornfield who is friendly and welcoming to Jane. She displays no false superiority towards Jane, but regards her as an equal. She is not very stimulating company, lacking both wit and humour and her outlook is conventional. This is why she warns Jane against marrying Mr Rochester – because of the social differences between them.

Mrs Reed

She is an unpleasant woman whose dislike of Jane and whose cruelty towards her is based on jealousy. But she is a weak woman and Jane is able to get the better of her before leaving Gateshead. We see her again at the end of her life, her premature death partly occasioned by the worry of a wayward son and two unloving daughters. Although she has called Jane to rectify the wrongs she has done to her in the past, there is no reconciliation and she dies still hating Jane.

St John Rivers

St John is classically handsome, but emotionally cold and reserved. Although he is kind and very dutiful he is also impatient with his present way of life. His ambition is to serve God as a missionary, although it is questionable whether it is the Almighty or his own ego that he is serving. He holds a steely control over his feelings, and, whilst admitting to being attracted to Rosamond, he will not do anything about it because she does not fit into his plans to serve God. Rosamond Oliver has beauty and wealth and, although highly conscious of both, manages not to become spoilt by them. She is pleasant and amusing but she is not very profound or serious. It is doubtful if she would make a good wife for a missionary, although it seems clear that there is some depth of emotion between her and St John Rivers.

St John wields enormous influence over Jane who is in awe of his Christian righteousness. He is a good man who seems motivated by all the wrong reasons; his fault is not seeing that other people must achieve goodness in their own way. He is intolerant, overbearing, and blinkered.

What happens in each chapter

Chapter 1   Jane is a young child living in her aunt's house at Gateshead. She is well-read and knowledgeable but is unloved and cruelly treated by her aunt and her cousins. Although she is acutely aware of her isolated position, she shows a determination to stand up for herself and fight for her independence.

Chapter 2   Put in the red-room as punishment, Jane is outraged at the injustice of her treatment at Gateshead. As her anger subsides she begins to consider death and, in particular, her uncle who died in that room. A play of light on the wall, coupled with her vivid imagination, convinces her of the arrival of a ghost. Her subsequent terror is dismissed by Mrs Reed, who locks her back in the room. At this point Jane loses consciousness. The supernatural, as a theme which recurs throughout the book, makes its appearance with this event.

Chapter 3   Jane's experience in the red-room leaves her feeling desperately miserable, although she does find that Bessie is more sympathetic to her now. The idea of sending her away to school is raised by Mr Lloyd the apothecary, and Jane overhears that Mrs Reed agrees. From the servants she also discovers the details of her own family background.

Chapter 4   After three months of even greater isolation, Jane is called to meet Mr Brocklehurst, who is the director of Lowood School. Her lack of piety fails to impress him and her character is further blackened by Mrs Reed. Enraged by the untruthfulness of Mrs Reed's remarks to Mr Brocklehurst, Jane challenges her and manages to frighten her. Her sense of victory over her cruel aunt is short-lived and she soon returns to her previous state of misery, comforted only by Bessie.

Chapter 5   Jane arrives at Lowood and tries to take in all the impressions of the first day. She notices the noise, the regimentation, the poor food. She likes Miss Temple and makes friends with Helen Burns, who is a serious girl. Her state of confusion is echoed in the wet, windy weather outside.

Chapter 6   Jane's impetuous, untrained character is contrasted with the humble, patient character of Helen. The latter epitomizes Christian tolerance and a belief that earthly injustices can be endured with the support of thoughts of the spiritual happiness which follows death.

Chapter 7   Cold and hunger are constant conditions of life at Lowood during Jane's first winter there. Mr Brocklehurst's dreaded visit takes place three weeks after her arrival. His cruelty and hypocrisy dominate the event and his visit culminates in Jane's public humiliation. Thanks to Helen's influence she is able to conquer her instincts and cope with it calmly.

Chapter 8   Jane comes to terms with life at Lowood and finds it preferable to Gateshead. She learns to endure the poor conditions because of the friendship of Helen and Miss Temple, particularly as the latter takes steps to clear her name. She is beginning to see the virtue in Helen's patience and tolerance, but her passionate nature still erupts in the face of injustice.

Chapter 9   The coming of spring and the typhus epidemic both conspire to improve conditions for those pupils fortunate enough to remain healthy. More freedom and better food make school life quite pleasant. Helen faces her own death peacefully, certain of her life to come with God in Heaven. Jane, who is so immersed in the present and in the joys of nature, is not so certain.

Chapter 10   Lowood changes for the better after the typhus epidemic, and Jane continues to live there contentedly for eight further years, the last two as a teacher. Miss Temple's eventual departure leaves her feeling restless, so she finds a new position as a governess. She is more than fit for the post, having acquired all the accomplishments of a lady, as Bessie confirms on her visit to Lowood.

Chapter 11   Jane is greeted warmly on her arrival at Thornfield and she is pleased to learn that Mrs Fairfax is not the owner, but the housekeeper. Jane finds this equal relationship preferable. She meets her pupil, Adèle, who turns out to be a lively, extrovert child, who is, however, unused to schooling. Mr Rochester's name is mentioned, but Jane learns little about him, although her curiosity is aroused. The chapter ends on a mysterious note – quite in contrast to its cheerful beginning.

Chapter 12   Jane begins to feel restless at Thornfield. Her duties as governess and the company of Mrs Fairfax cannot prevent her growing desire to experience more of life. All this is a prelude to her meeting with Mr Rochester, which occurs unexpectedly and anonymously. The features of their final relationship are present from the beginning – their instant and instinctive interest in each other, their mutual dependence and the aura of mystery and the overtones of the supernatural which surround that relationship.

Chapter 13   Thornfield seems a more cheerful place now that Mr Rochester is there. Jane is summoned to meet him and, although she finds his manner abrupt, she is not frightened of him. Their conversation is lighthearted and he is clearly impressed by her artistic talents. Later Mrs Fairfax reveals the mystery surrounding Mr Rochester's background; this seems to account for much of his moodiness.

Chapter 14   Jane and Mr Rochester continue their acquaintance and despite his ungraciousness, Jane is not put off. In fact her frankness surprises him. The traditional master-servant relationship is dispensed with when Jane makes it apparent that she will not speak to order. This gives room for a more personal relationship to grow between them and the first signs of this are already present. Mr Rochester, who sees himself as a character soiled by experience and fortune, is attracted to the innocence of Jane. Jane, who in Mr Rochester's company is at the moment prim and serious, grows increasingly confident as her natural passion surfaces.

Chapter 15   Jane learns the truth about Adèle's origins and is told the full story about Céline Varens. Jane finds a new sympathy for Adèle now that she knows about her background. The mystery of Thornfield deepens as Rochester reveals his strange and profound antipathy towards the house. Jane is pondering this mystery when, late one night, she hears laughter. On investigation, she discovers Rochester's bed is on fire. The incident brings them closer together and makes them conscious of their love for each other.

Chapter 16   Jane is surprised to hear of Rochester's departure. She is disappointed not to be able to question him about the previous night's event of the burning bed. When she finds out where he is and learns about Blanche Ingram she realizes that it is folly for her to believe that Rochester should have any special feeling for her. To discipline herself she draws her own portrait in chalk and paints a miniature of Blanche in oils, then sets one up in comparison with the other.

Chapter 17   Mr Rochester returns with a party of guests, one of whom is Blanche Ingram. Grace Poole still intrigues Jane and although she hears more details about her, Jane feels she is not being told everything. Adèle is excited by the prospect of guests in the house and is overwhelmed at the sight of such glamorous people. Jane and Adèle are summoned to the drawing-room the next night and they are able to observe these society people at first hand. Jane is struck by the elaborateness of their costumes and the haughtiness of their faces. She is particularly observant of Blanche of course, whom she finds beautiful but proud. She has time to observe Mr Rochester too, and reflect on her feelings for him. She has to admit that she loves him. The attention of the guests is drawn to Jane as they discuss governesses, not in a very flattering way. While Mr

Rochester and Blanche are singing Jane leaves quietly but she is stopped in the corridor by Mr Rochester, who tells her he expects her to be present every evening whilst his guests remain.

Chapter 18   As a diversion one day the house party play charades. This is a delightful touch of irony on Brontë's part, as the game mirrors the artificial nature of their behaviour. The scenes they act allude to weddings and prisons. Jane has time to observe Blanche and Rochester together. She realizes that if he marries her it will not be for love. The guests are surprised one day by the arrival of a man from the West Indies. An intriguing diversion is created at the end of the chapter by the entrance of a gypsy who wishes to tell their fortunes.

Chapter 19   Jane meets the fortune-telling gypsy but makes it clear from the start that she is very sceptical. The gypsy tries to find out her thoughts about Mr Rochester and Blanche Ingram, but she carefully avoids any revealing answers. The gypsy implicitly forecasts Jane's reaction to the identity of Bertha Rochester and we glimpse the possibilities of a plan that seems to be forming in Mr Rochester's mind. Jane is relatively unsurprised when Mr Rochester reveals himself as the 'gypsy', although she is vexed at the deception. He is deeply shocked when told of Mr Mason's arrival although he seems in better spirits later, at bedtime.

Chapter 20   Blood-curdling cries awaken the household. Rochester, having reassured the guests that all is well, asks Jane to come up to the attics. There, she finds Mason badly wounded. She tends his injuries until Rochester returns with a doctor. They administer immediate help but insist that he must depart by daybreak. Rochester and Jane go into the garden where he alludes to his past life and is on the point of confessing his love when he changes the subject and begins to discuss instead his proposed marriage to Blanche Ingram.

Chapter 21   Dreams of children mean trouble, according to Bessie. After one such dream Jane is summoned to Gateshead, where her aunt is dying. Overcoming Rochester's reluctance to let her go, and having made a stand about keeping her independent, financial position, Jane makes her way to Gateshead; there she finds Eliza and Georgiana, opposites in both looks and personalities but equally unfriendly and indifferent to her presence. Her aunt, unchanged in her feelings for Jane, has called her out of a sense of guilt. She confesses that she had lied to Jane's uncle who wanted her to inherit his fortune. This interlude at Gateshead underlines a maturity of character in Jane. Not only is she able to withstand the coldness of her cousins but is also ready to forgive her aunt for the injustices she has done her.

Chapter 22   After delaying at Gateshead because of the selfish demands of her cousins, Jane begins the journey home. She is unsure how she will feel going back and also unsure for how long she will be remaining there. She is convinced of the certainty of Rochester's forthcoming marriage to Blanche and she steels herself to face it. She arrives at Thornfield on a balmy summer's evening and sees Rochester in the garden. She loses all control over her passion and is overwhelmed by her love for him. Unwillingly, she allows Rochester to sense this. She is delighted by her warm reception from everyone at Thornfield and settles back into the routine, nursing the hope that she will be kept on as governess after Rochester's marriage. Strangely, though, there is no more talk of weddings and Rochester makes no further visits to Blanche.

Chapter 23   It is midsummer's day and there is an air of ripeness and perfection in the countryside. Jane and Rochester meet in the garden at the 'sweetest' hour of the day. He discloses his plan to send her to Ireland, but the thought of never seeing him again makes her lose control, break down, and declare her love for him. This done, he is able to confess his true feelings. The moment of perfection is broken by a change in the weather and the beginnings of a storm. The chestnut tree is struck by lightning and it splits in two, a symbol of the fate which will overtake Jane and Rochester.

Chapter 24   After the declaration of their mutual love Jane has to make great efforts to ensure her independence. She shuns all talk of fine clothes and jewels and wishes to maintain her status of governess as well as her financial independence. She makes clear her disapproval of the way Rochester has misused Blanche Ingram and criticizes his lack of principle. She is upset by Mrs Fairfax's cool reception to the news of their forthcoming marriage. Her strong desire for independence makes her decide to write to her uncle about her inheritance. Unwittingly, by doing so, she has sown the seeds of disaster. Her behaviour towards Rochester is offhand as she wishes to keep a distance between them before the marriage, partly for the sake of establishing her own independence but also out of an awareness of the dangers of the strong feelings they have for each other.

Chapter 25   Jane is agitated and her mood is matched by the turbulent weather. She wanders in the garden and sees the damaged chestnut tree. Jane is filled with a sense of foreboding and she longs for Rochester's return so that she can reveal to him the cause of her troubled mind. She relates her two dreams to him, which seem to her to be presentiments of disaster. Then she tells of the fearful apparition in her room. Rochester suggests that it must have been Grace Poole she saw, who looked frightening because of Jane's fevered imagination. She believes him and retires to bed in calmer mood.

Chapter 26   In unusual haste Mr Rochester leads Jane to the church. Reference is made to, but little account taken of, two shadowy figures in the churchyard. They are responsible for bringing the marriage to a halt and the truth about the existence of Mr Rochester's wife is revealed. Jane is taken to visit Bertha in her attic room where she is seen behaving more like a wild animal than a human being. Jane's first reaction to the events of the day is numbness, but gradually she is filled with a sense of betrayal and a huge wave of despair pours over her.

Chapter 27   Jane struggles between the dictates of her conscience and the pull of her feelings. She feels friendless and alone but realizes that she must leave Thornfield. Rochester has not even considered the possibility of her going. He is quite sure that a true account of his doomed marriage will convince her of their right to be together – but he is wrong. Nothing will change her mind; she must be true to herself and do as her conscience says. As a result of a dream where a voice urges her to leave, she sets off, unseen, early the next morning.

Chapter 28   Left by the coachman in the middle of the countryside, Jane's sense of isolation is complete. She enjoys the contact with nature and would be happy to stay were it not for the practicalities of finding food and lodging. Against her will she is reduced to begging and after two miserable days, when even nature seems against her, she has the good fortune to be taken in by the Rivers family.

Chapter 29   It takes Jane four days to recover from her state of starvation and exhaustion. She is well received by Diana and Mary although Hannah, the servant, is at first resentful of her. Hannah gives her details of the Rivers' family background. St John, although classically handsome, is cold and reserved. When he does question Jane about her past he shows little sensitivity to her awkwardness and embarrassment. She admits she has given them a false name but refuses to reveal her true one. The two girls are willing to accept her for what she is. St John is not so open although he agrees to try to find her some occupation.

Chapter 30   Living with the Rivers girls at Moor House is a pleasant experience for Jane, as they have so much in common. St John is more reserved and she senses in him a dissatisfaction with his present life. Diana and Mary prepare to go back to their posts as governesses. St John asks Jane to take on the post as village schoolmistress. Despite its low status, she accepts the job because it gives her shelter and independence. The Rivers learn of the death of their uncle, which is a more significant event than any of them yet realize.

Chapter 31   Although Jane does not look upon her work as schoolmistress with any great enthusiasm she is grateful for a home and hopes that improvement in her pupils will bring her satisfaction. The vexed question of whether she should be obedient to her own nature or to the laws of God is considered first from Jane's point of view, then from St John's. Jane is not sure that she did the right thing by leaving Thornfield. St John is quite sure that obeying God's will is the right thing, and yet at what cost? His encounter with Miss Oliver reveals the price he pays.

Chapter 32   Jane becomes accepted in the village and finds her job more tolerable than it was initially. On the surface life is tranquil but she is plagued by disturbing dreams of Rochester. She is intrigued by the curious relationship between Miss Oliver and St John and, having established that both Miss Oliver and her father are in favour of a match, she tackles St John on the subject. He will only admit to a superficial regard for Miss Oliver, whom he argues would, in any case, not make him a suitable wife. He repeats his determination to serve God as a missionary, thus ensuring his place in Heaven. He leaves Jane and, as he goes, mysteriously tears a corner off a piece of paper on which she has been drawing.

Chapter 33   Jane hears of the fortune which she has inherited, and of her link with the Rivers family. She is glad of the independence her fortune will bring her but she is even more thrilled to know she has cousins – a real family. With difficulty she persuades the others each to accept a quarter of her fortune.

Chapter 34   Jane shuts the school and settles back to life in Moor House, which she prepares for the return of Diana and Mary. St John disapproves of her apparently having nothing better to do than domestic chores, and he presses her to use her talents more profitably. It becomes clear to Jane that St John finds domestic life distasteful and that he cannot wait to begin his life as a missionary. He begins to influence Jane, suggesting he teach her 'Hindostanee', and she finds herself behaving in a way which, although pleasing to him, suppresses half of her true nature. She is not happy about this but sees no way to overcome it. St John is still cold towards her and yet he asks her to be his wife. She agrees to come to India as a 'sister', but refuses to marry him because of her conviction that a marriage without love would be totally against her nature. St John stubbornly persists, arrogantly suggesting that it is God's will that he is carrying out. She becomes conscious of this stance as a flaw in his character and is therefore finally able to detect the man behind the Christian. This gives her strength to be her normal self again and she is able to throw off the 'fetters' of his domination and say what she truly thinks.

Chapter 35   St John behaves very coldly to Jane after she has argued with him, not out of spite but because he believes she is in the wrong. She regrets this because she valued his friendship. Jane repeats that she will go to India only as a sister, but he will not accept this and is angry. She repeats that to marry him would kill her and she emphasizes that she feels no sense of dishonour because she had not promised unconditionally to go. She admits that she still has the desire to find out what happened to Rochester, a notion which St John censures. Diana agrees that St John and Jane are unsuited. Her resolve weakens again when she comes under his clerical influence and in a state of turmoil she says she will agree if it is 'God's will'. As if in demonstration of what is truly God's will, she hears Rochester's voice calling out her name.

Chapter 36   Stirred by the voice of Mr Rochester, Jane determines to return to Thornfield and discover his whereabouts. On reaching Thornfield she finds that it is a blackened ruin. At the inn she is told how Bertha set fire to it, and was herself then killed. She also learns that Mr Rochester was injured, and lives now at Ferndean, his other home, and is both blind and otherwise maimed.

Chapter 37   Jane arrives at Ferndean, a solitary place buried deep in the countryside, and observes Rochester in the garden. His face has changed, and he looks sullen and brooding. Later she goes in to see him, unannounced, and he is incredulous. She informs him of her new-found financial independence. She also has a new confidence with him and we are aware of the shifts in their relationship as they get to know each other again. *She* is the one that teases, *she* is the one who makes him jealous. He is the one that is reticent to ask her to marry him, but when he does he wants to marry without fuss or finery. He has been humbled by misfortune, and finds that he is more dependent on Jane. However, there is a greater degree of equality between them. He is beginning to see the hand of God in all things.

Chapter 38   All the loose ends are resolved. We hear what happens to Adèle, to Mary and Diana, and to St John. Most of all we learn of Jane's and Rochester's marital bliss and of the good fortune of a partial restoration of his sight, for 'God had tempered judgement with mercy'.

Coursework and preparing for the examination

If you wish to gain a certificate in English literature then there is no substitute for studying the text/s on which you are to be examined. If you cannot be bothered to do that, then neither this guide nor any other will be of use to you.

Here we give advice on studying the text, writing a good essay, producing coursework, and sitting the examination. However, if you meet problems you should ask your teacher for help.

Studying the text

No, not just read–study. You must read your text at least twice. Do not dismiss it if you find a first reading difficult or uninteresting. Approach the text with an open mind and you will often find a second reading more enjoyable. When you become a more experienced reader enjoyment usually follows from a close study of the text, when you begin to appreciate both what the author is saying and the skill with which it is said.

Having read the text, you must now study it. We restrict our remarks here to novels and plays, though much of what is said can also be applied to poetry.

1 You will know in full detail all the major incidents in your text, **why**, **where** and **when** they happen, **who** is involved, **what** leads up to them and what follows.

2 You must show that you have an **understanding of the story**, the **characters**, and the **main ideas** which the author is exploring.

3 In a play you must know what happens in each act, and more specifically the organization of the scene structure–how one follows from and builds upon another. Dialogue in both plays and novels is crucial. You must have a detailed knowledge of the major dialogues and soliloquies and the part they play in the development of plot, and the development and drawing of character.

4 When you write about a novel you will not normally be expected to quote or to refer to specific lines but references to incidents and characters must be given, and they must be accurate and specific.

5 In writing about a play you will be expected both to paraphrase dialogue and quote specific lines, always provided, of course, that they are actually contributing something to your essay!

To gain full marks in coursework and/or in an examination you will also be expected to show your own reaction to, and appreciation of, the text studied. The teacher or examiner always welcomes those essays which demonstrate the student's own thoughtful response to the text. Indeed, questions often specify such a requirement, so do participate in those classroom discussions, the debates, class dramatizations of all or selected parts of your text, and the many other activities which enable a class to share and grow in their understanding and feeling for literature.

Making notes
A half-hearted reading of your text, or watching the 'film of the book' will not give you the necessary knowledge to meet the above demands.

As you study the text jot down sequences of events; quotations of note; which events precede and follow the part you are studying; the characters involved; what the part being studied contributes to the plot and your understanding of character and ideas.

Write single words, phrases and short sentences which can be quickly reviewed and which will help you to gain a clear picture of the incident being studied. Make your notes neat and orderly, with headings to indicate chapter, scene, page, incident, character, etc, so that you can quickly find the relevant notes or part of the text when revising.

Writing the essay

Good essays are like good books, in miniature; they are thought about, planned, logically structured, paragraphed, have a clearly defined pattern and development of thought, and are presented clearly – and with neat writing! All of this will be to no avail if the tools you use, i.e. words, and the skill with which you put them together to form your sentences and paragraphs are severely limited.

How good is your general and literary vocabulary? Do you understand and can you make appropriate use of such terms as 'soliloquy', 'character', 'plot', 'mood', 'dramatically effective', 'comedy', 'allusion', 'humour', 'imagery', 'irony', 'paradox', 'anti-climax', 'tragedy'? These are all words which examiners have commented on as being misunderstood by students.

Do you understand 'metaphor', 'simile', 'alliteration'? Can you say what their effect is on you, the reader, and how they enable the author to express himself more effectively than by the use of a different literary device? If you cannot, you are employing your time ineffectively by using them.

You are writing an English literature essay and your writing should be literate and appropriate. Slang, colloquialisms and careless use of words are not tolerated in such essays.

Essays for coursework
The exact number of essays you will have to produce and their length will vary; it depends upon the requirements of the examination board whose course you are following, and whether you will be judged solely on coursework or on a mixture of coursework and examination.

As a guide, however your course is structured, you will be required to provide a folder containing at least ten essays, and from that folder approximately five will be selected for moderation purposes. Of those essays, one will normally have been done in class-time under conditions similar to those of an examination. The essays must cover the complete range of course requirements and be the unaided work of the student. One board specifies that these pieces of continuous writing should be a minimum of 400 words long, and another, a minimum of 500 words long. Ensure that you know what is required for your course, and do not aim for the minimum amount – write a full essay then prune it down if necessary.

Do take care over the presentation of your final folder of coursework. There are many devices on the market which will enable you to bind your work neatly, and in such a way that you can easily insert new pieces. Include a 'Contents' page and a front and back cover to keep your work clean. Ring binders are unsuitable items to hand in for **final** assessment purposes as they are much too bulky.

What sort of coursework essays will you be set? All boards lay down criteria similar to the following for the range of student response to literature that the coursework must cover.

Work must demonstrate that the student:

1 shows an understanding not only of surface meaning but also of a deeper awareness of themes and attitudes;

2 recognizes and appreciates ways in which authors use language;

3 recognizes and appreciates ways in which writers achieve their effects, particularly in how the work is structured and in its characterization;

4 can write imaginatively in exploring and developing ideas so as to communicate a sensitive and informed personal response to what is read.

Much of what is said in the section **'Writing essays in an examination'** (below) is relevant here, but for coursework essays you have the advantage of plenty of time to prepare your work – so take advantage of it.

There is no substitute for arguing, discussing and talking about a question on a particular text or theme. Your teacher should give you plenty of opportunity for this in the classroom. Listening to what others say about a subject often opens up for you new ways to look at and respond to it. The same can be said for reading about a topic. Be careful not to copy down slavishly what others say and write. Jot down notes then go away and think about what you have heard, read and written. Make more notes of your own and then start to clarify your own thoughts, feelings and emotions on the subject about which you are writing. Most students make the mistake of doing their coursework essays in a rush – you have time so use it.

Take a great deal of care in planning your work. From all your notes, write a rough draft and then start the task of really perfecting it.

1 Look at your arrangement of paragraphs, is there a logical development of thought or argument? Do the paragraphs need rearranging in order? Does the first or last sentence of any paragraph need redrafting in order to provide a sensible link with the preceding or next paragraph?

2 Look at the pattern of sentences within each paragraph. Are your thoughts and ideas clearly developed and expressed? Have you used any quotations, paraphrases, or references to incidents to support your opinions and ideas? Are those references relevant and apt, or just 'padding'?

3 Look at the words you have used. Try to avoid repeating words in close proximity one to another. Are the words you have used to comment on the text being studied the most appropriate and effective, or just the first ones you thought of?

4 Check your spelling and punctuation.

5 Now write a final draft, the quality of which should reflect the above considerations.

Writing essays in an examination
Read the question. Identify the key words and phrases. Write them down, and as they are dealt with in your essay plan, tick them off.

Plan your essay. Spend about five minutes jotting down ideas; organize your thoughts and ideas into a logical and developing order – a structure is essential to the production of a good essay. Remember, brief, essential notes only!

Write your essay
How long should it be? There is no magic length. What you must do is answer the question set, fully and sensitively in the time allowed. You will probably have about forty minutes to answer an essay question, and within that time you should produce an essay between roughly 350 and 500 words in length. Very short answers will not do justice to the question, very long answers will probably contain much irrelevant information and waste time that should be spent on the next answer.

How much quotation? Use only that which is apt and contributes to the clarity and quality of your answer. No examiner will be impressed by 'padding'.

What will the examiners be looking for in an essay?
1 An answer to the question set, and not a prepared answer to another, albeit slightly similar question done in class.

2 A well-planned, logically structured and paragraphed essay with a beginning, middle and end.

3 Accurate references to plot, character, theme, as required by the question.

4 Appropriate, brief, and if needed, frequent quotation and references to support and demonstrate the comments that you are making in your essay.

5 Evidence that reading the text has prompted in you a personal response to it, as well as some judgment and appreciation of its literary merit.

How do you prepare to do this?
1 During your course you should write between three to five essays on each text.

2 Make good use of class discussion etc, as mentioned in a previous paragraph on page 75.

3 Try to see a live performance of a play. It may help to see a film of a play or book, though be aware that directors sometimes leave out episodes, change their order, or worse, add episodes that are not in the original – so be very careful. In the end, there is no substitute for **reading and studying** the text!

Try the following exercises without referring to any notes or text.

1 Pick a character from your text.

2 Make a list of his/her qualities – both positive and negative ones, or aspects that you cannot quite define. Jot down single words to describe each quality. If you do not know the word you want, use a thesaurus, but use it in conjunction with a dictionary and make sure you are fully aware of the meaning of each word you use.

3 Write a short sentence which identifies one or more places in the text where you think each quality is demonstrated.

4 Jot down any brief quotation, paraphrase of conversation or outline of an incident which shows that quality.

5 Organize the list. Identify groupings which contrast the positive and negative aspects of character.

6 Write a description of that character which makes full use of the material you have just prepared.

7 What do you think of the character you have just described? How has he/she reacted to and coped with the pressures of the other characters, incidents, and the setting of the story? Has he/she changed in any way? In no more than 100 words, including 'evidence' taken from the text, write a balanced assessment of the character, and draw some conclusions.

You should be able to do the above without notes, and without the text, unless you are to take an examination which allows the use of plain texts. In plain text examinations you are allowed to take in a copy of your text. It must be without notes, either your own or the publisher's. The intention is to enable you to consult a text in the examination so as to confirm memory of detail, thus enabling a candidate to quote and refer more accurately in order to illustrate his/her views that more effectively. Examiners will expect a high standard of accurate reference, quotation and comment in a plain text examination.

Sitting the examination

You will have typically between two and five essays to write and you will have roughly 40 minutes, on average, to write each essay.

On each book you have studied, you should have a choice of doing at least one out of two or three essay titles set.

1 **Before sitting the exam**, make sure you are completely clear in your mind that you know exactly how many questions you must answer, which sections of the paper you must tackle, and how many questions you may, or must, attempt on any one book or in any one section of the paper. If you are not sure, ask your teacher.

2 **Always read the instructions** given at the top of your examination paper. They are

there to help you. Take your time, and try to relax – panicking will not help.

3 **Be very clear about timing, and organizing your time.**

(a) Know how long the examination is.
(b) Know how many questions you must do.
(c) Divide (b) into (a) to work out how long you may spend on each question. (Bear in mind that some questions may attract more marks, and should therefore take proportionately more time.)
(d) Keep an eye on the time, and do not spend more than you have allowed for any one question.
(e) If you have spare time at the end you can come back to a question and do more work on it.
(f) Do not be afraid to jot down notes as an aid to memory, but do cross them out carefully after use – a single line will do!

4 **Do not rush the decision** as to which question you are going to answer on a particular text.

(a) Study each question carefully.
(b) Be absolutely sure what each one is asking for.
(c) Make your decision as to which you will answer.

5 **Having decided which question** you will attempt:

(a) jot down the key points of the actual question – use single words or short phrases;
(b) think about how you are going to arrange your answer. Five minutes here, with some notes jotted down will pay dividends later;
(c) write your essay, and keep an eye on the time!

6 **Adopt the same approach** for all questions. Do write answers for the maximum number of questions you are told to attempt. One left out will lose its proportion of the total marks. Remember also, you will never be awarded extra marks, over and above those already allocated, if you write an extra long essay on a particular question.

7 **Do not waste time** on the following:

(a) an extra question – you will get no marks for it;
(b) worrying about how much anyone else is writing, they can't help you!
(c) relaxing at the end with time to spare – you do not have any. Work up to the very moment the invigilator tells you to stop writing. Check and recheck your work, including spelling and punctuation. Every single mark you gain helps, and that last mark might tip the balance between success and failure – the line has to be drawn somewhere.

8 **Help the examiner.**

(a) Do not use red or green pen or pencil on your paper. Examiners usually annotate your script in red and green, and if you use the same colours it will cause unnecessary confusion.
(b) Leave some space between each answer or section of an answer. This could also help you if you remember something you wish to add to your answer when you are checking it.
(c) Number your answers as instructed. If it is question 3 you are doing, do not label it 'C'.
(d) Write neatly. It will help you to communicate effectively with the examiner who is trying to read your script.

Glossary of literary terms

Mere knowledge of the words in this list or other specialist words used when studying literature is not sufficient. You must know when to use a particular term, and be able to describe what it contributes to that part of the work which is being discussed.

For example, merely to label something as being a metaphor does not help an examiner or teacher to assess your response to the work being studied. You must go on to analyse what the literary device contributes to the work. Why did the author use a metaphor at all? Why not some other literary device? What extra sense of feeling or meaning does the metaphor convey to the reader? How effective is it in supporting the author's intention? What was the author's intention, as far as you can judge, in using that metaphor?

Whenever you use a particular literary term you must do so with a purpose and that purpose usually involves an explanation and expansion upon its use. Occasionally you will simply use a literary term 'in passing', as, for example, when you refer to the 'narrator' of a story as opposed to the 'author' – they are not always the same! So please be sure that you understand both the meaning and purpose of each literary term you employ.

This list includes only those words which we feel will assist in helping you to understand the major concepts in play and novel construction. It makes no attempt to be comprehensive. These are the concepts which examiners frequently comment upon as being inadequately grasped by many students. Your teacher will no doubt expand upon this list and introduce you to other literary devices and words within the context of the particular work/s you are studying – the most useful place to experience and explore them and their uses.

Plot This is the plan or story of a play or novel. Just as a body has a skeleton to hold it together, so the plot forms the 'bare bones' of the work of literature in play or novel form. It is however, much more than this. It is arranged in time, so one of the things which encourages us to continue reading is to see what happens next. It deals with causality, that is how one event or incident causes another. It has a sequence, so that in general, we move from the beginning through to the end.

Structure The arrangement and interrelationship of parts in a play or novel are obviously bound up with the plot. An examination of how the author has structured his work will lead us to consider the function of, say, the 43 letters which are such an important part of *Pride and Prejudice*. We would consider the arrangement of the time-sequence in *Wuthering Heights* with its 'flashbacks' and their association with the different narrators of the story. In a play we would look at the scene divisions and how different events are placed in a relationship so as to produce a particular effect; where soliloquies occur so as to inform the audience of a character's innermost emotions and feelings. Do be aware that great works of fiction are not just simply thrown together by their authors. We study a work in detail, admiring its parts and the intricacies of its structure. The reason for a work's greatness has to do with the genius of its author and the care of its construction. Ultimately, though, we do well to remember that it is the work as a whole that we have to judge, not just the parts which make up that whole.

Narrator A narrator tells or relates a story. In *Wuthering Heights* various characters take on the task of narrating the events of the story: Cathy, Heathcliff, etc, as well as being, at other times, central characters taking their part in the story. Sometimes the author will be there, as it were, in person, relating and explaining events. The method adopted in telling the story relates very closely to style and structure.

Style The manner in which something is expressed or performed, considered as separate from its intrinsic content or meaning. It might well be that a lyrical, almost poetical style will be used, for example concentrating on the beauties and contrasts of the natural world as a foil to the narration of the story and creating emotions in the reader which serve to heighten reactions to the events being played out on the page. It might be that the author uses a terse, almost staccato approach to the conveyance of his story. There is no simple route to grasping the variations of style which are to be found between different authors or indeed within one novel. The surest way to appreciate this difference is to read widely and thoughtfully and to analyse and appreciate the various strategies which an author uses to command our attention.

Character A person represented in a play or story. However, the word also refers to the combination of traits and qualities distinguishing the individual nature of a person or thing. Thus, a characteristic is one such distinguishing quality: in *Pride and Prejudice*, the pride and prejudices of various characters are central to the novel, and these characteristics which are associated with Mr Darcy, Elizabeth, and Lady Catherine in that novel, enable us to begin assessing how a character is reacting to the surrounding events and people. Equally, the lack of a particular trait or characteristic can also tell us much about a character.

Character development In *Pride and Prejudice*, the extent to which Darcy's pride, or Elizabeth's prejudice is altered, the recognition by those characters of such change, and the events of the novel which bring about the changes are central to any exploration of how a character develops, for better or worse.

Irony This is normally taken to be the humorous or mildly sarcastic use of words to imply the opposite of what they say. It also refers to situations and events and thus you will come across references such as prophetic, tragic, and dramatic irony.

Dramatic irony This occurs when the implications of a situation or speech are understood by the audience but not by all or some of the characters in the play or novel. We also class as ironic words spoken innocently but which a later event proves either to have been mistaken or to have prophesied that event. When we read in the play *Macbeth*:

> *Macbeth*
> Tonight we hold a solemn supper, sir,
> And I'll request your presence.

> *Banquo*
> Let your highness
> Command upon me, to the which my duties
> Are with a most indissoluble tie
> Forever knit.

we, as the audience, will shortly have revealed to us the irony of Macbeth's words. He does not expect Banquo to attend the supper as he plans to have Banquo murdered before the supper occurs. However, what Macbeth does not know is the prophetic irony of Banquo's response. His 'duties. . . a most indissoluble tie' will be fulfilled by his appearance at the supper as a ghost – something Macbeth certainly did not forsee or welcome, and which Banquo most certainly did not have in mind!

Tragedy This is usually applied to a play in which the main character, usually a person of importance and outstanding personal qualities, falls to disaster through the combination of personal failing and circumstances with which he cannot deal. Such tragic happenings may also be central to a novel. In *The Mayor of Casterbridge*, flaws in Henchard's character are partly responsible for his downfall and eventual death.

In Shakespeare's plays, *Macbeth* and *Othello*, the tragic heroes from which the two plays take their names, are both highly respected and honoured men who have proven their outstanding personal qualities. Macbeth, driven on by his ambition and that of his very determined wife, kills his king. It leads to civil war in his country, to his own eventual downfall and death, and to his wife's suicide. Othello, driven to an insane jealousy by the cunning of his lieutenant, Iago, murders his own innocent wife and commits suicide.

Satire   Where topical issues, folly or evil are held up to scorn by means of ridicule and irony – the satire may be subtle or openly abusive.

In *Animal Farm*, George Orwell used the rebellion of the animals against their oppressive owner to satirize the excesses of the Russian revolution at the beginning of the 20th century. It would be a mistake, however, to see the satire as applicable only to that event. There is a much wider application of that satire to political and social happenings both before and since the Russian revolution and in all parts of the world.

Images   An image is a mental representation or picture. One that constantly recurs in *Macbeth* is clothing, sometimes through double meanings of words: 'he seems rapt withal', 'Why do you dress me in borrowed robes?', 'look how our partner's rapt', 'Like our strange garments, cleave not to their mould', 'Whiles I stood rapt in the wonder of it', 'which would be worn now in their newest gloss', 'Was the hope drunk Wherein you dressed yourself?', 'Lest our old robes sit easier than our new.', 'like a giant's robe upon a dwarfish thief'. All these images serve to highlight and comment upon aspects of Macbeth's behaviour and character. In Act 5, Macbeth the loyal soldier who was so honoured by his king at the start of the play, struggles to regain some small shred of his self-respect. Three times he calls to Seyton for his armour, and finally moves toward his destiny with the words 'Blow wind, come wrack, At least we'll die with harness on our back' – his own armour, not the borrowed robes of a king he murdered.

Do remember that knowing a list of images is not sufficient. You must be able to interpret them and comment upon the contribution they make to the story being told.

Theme   A unifying idea, image or motif, repeated or developed throughout a work.

In *Pride and Prejudice*, a major theme is marriage. During the course of the novel we are shown various views of and attitudes towards marriage. We actually witness the relationships of four different couples through their courtship, engagement and eventual marriage. Through those events and the examples presented to us in the novel of other already married couples, the author engages in a thorough exploration of the theme.

This list is necessarily short. There are whole books devoted to the explanation of literary terms. Some concepts, like style, need to be experienced and discussed in a group setting with plenty of examples in front of you. Others, such as dramatic irony, need keen observation from the student and a close knowledge of the text to appreciate their significance and existence. All such specialist terms are well worth knowing. But they should be used only if they enable you to more effectively express your knowledge and appreciation of the work being studied.